Shriven Selves

Shriven Selves

Religious Problems in Recent American Fiction

Wesley A. Kort

Fortress Press   Philadelphia

Grateful acknowledgment is made to the following publishers for permission to quote from the indicated works:

To Doubleday & Company, Inc., New York, New York, for quotations from J. F. Powers, *Morte D'Urban,* copyright © 1956, 1957, 1960, 1962 by James F. Powers.

To Little, Brown and Company, Boston, Massachusetts, for quotations from Peter De Vries, *The Blood of the Lamb,* copyright © 1961 by Peter De Vries.

To Alfred A. Knopf, Inc., New York, New York, for quotations from John Updike, *The Centaur,* copyright © 1963 by John Updike.

To Farrar, Straus & Giroux, Inc., New York, New York, for quotations from Bernard Malamud, *The Fixer,* copyright © 1966 by Bernard Malamud.

To Random House, Inc., New York, New York, for quotations from William A. Styron, *The Confessions of Nat Turner,* copyright © 1967 by William A. Styron.

To Farrar, Straus & Giroux, Inc., New York, New York, for quotations from Isaac Bashevis Singer, *The Magician of Lublin,* copyright © 1960 by Isaac Bashevis Singer.

To Harper & Row, Inc., New York, New York, for a quotation from Martin Buber, *Pointing the Way,* copyright © 1957 by Martin Buber.

Portions of this book also appeared, in a different form, in the July 1970 issue of the *Anglican Theological Review,* Evanston, Illinois, and are reprinted with permission.

Library of Congress Catalog Card Number 78–171499

ISBN (cloth) 0–8006–0408–3

ISBN (paper) 0–8006–0108–4

3038H71   Printed in the United States of America   1–108

The Reverend Arthur H. Kort

1893–1944

Ἄξιός ἐστιν τὸ ἀρνίον τὸ ἐσφαγμένον. . .

Contents

Preface   ix

Introduction: Recent Fiction and the Religious Situation   1

1. *Morte D'Urban* and the Presence of Clergy   15

2. *The Blood of the Lamb* and the Sense of
   Transcendent Power   36

3. *The Centaur* and the Problem of Vocation   64

4. *The Fixer* and the Death of God   90

5. *The Confessions of Nat Turner* and the
   Dynamic of Revolution   116

Conclusion: Abraham's Third Sons   141

Preface

The religious problems which give rise, shape, or strength to the works of fiction around which this study is ordered are problems deeply rooted in the religious life and thought which Americans inherit, and they are exacerbated by the present situation in which this religious heritage now lives. Responses to these problems within the fiction are highly personal, and they reflect what appears to be a growing form of contemporary spirituality.

This study, as it attempts to point to and discuss these matters, rests on two conclusions, one about the literature and the other about the religious situation. First, to speak about such problems and responses is not to neglect what is literary, formal, or aesthetic about the fiction because the nature of the problems and the form of the work in each case shape and enhance one another. Second, the religious problems which are discussed in this study are all related to a common dilemma, namely, the noninclusive character of the dominant religious forms of our time, a characteristic not limited to but aggravated by the present in which these forms are not expected or even permitted to be totally inclusive. These conclusions are drawn from the matters at hand, the fiction studied.

These conclusions constitute the completion point of a rather long journey, the turns and twists of which may still be recorded in this book. The time, then, is one for looking back with gratitude to those along the way who gave directions, encouragement, and help, people such as the late Cornelius Bontecoe and Henry Zylstra;

PREFACE

my teachers at Chicago, especially Preston T. Roberts and Nathan A. Scott; former colleagues at Princeton, particularly John Wilson and Victor Preller; my colleagues here at Duke, especially Roland Murphy and Harry Partin; and other friends, particularly Nelvin Vos and Patrick Sullivan. These are only a few from a large crowd of learned and stimulating people who, in their books and in conversation, gave to me far more than I could be counted on to handle well.

I also want to express my gratitude for institutions: for the University of Chicago where, free of charge, I was granted access to more than I was prepared to take; for Princeton University, my first employer, where I learned so much about the problems and possibilities of teaching religion; for Duke University which has opened itself to my work in religion and literature and which, through the Research Council, provided for some of the cost in preparing this manuscript; and, finally, for the Church which has taught me both the strengths and the limitations of its irreplaceable words and acts.

Finally, I want to thank those dearest to me for all that cannot and ought not to be mentioned.

Duke University, 1971

Introduction:

Recent Fiction and the
Religious Situation

When the protagonist of Isaac Singer's *The Magician of Lublin*,
Yasha Mazur, steps into the street after his rich experiences of
peace and refuge in the synagogue, he recognizes the separation of
what he had experienced a moment ago from what he now sees
before him. Worship and daily urban life seem to be not steps but
oceans apart. The narrator says:

> It now seemed to Yasha that the street and the synagogue denied
> each other. If one were true, then the other was certainly false. He
> understood that this was the voice of evil having its way, but the
> piety, which had consumed him as he stood in the prayer shawl
> and phylacteries in the prayer-house, began to cool now and
> evaporate.[1]

Yasha's sense of the conflict between his personal, religious life
and the public life of Warsaw is central to his problem. Throughout the work he suffers this conflict, and he resolves it at the end
not by electing one side but by rejecting both in favor of a brick
cell in which, freed from the tension, he can press forward to some
realization of himself as an integrated person.

The problem Yasha Mazur feels to his bones and his drastic
response to it constitute a difficulty and a strategy that mark the

---

1. Isaac B. Singer, *The Magician of Lublin,* trans. Elaine Gottlieb and
Joseph Singer (New York: Farrar, Straus and Cudahy, 1960), p. 155.

characters in recent American fiction over and over again. It is for the purpose of exposing this problem, its roots and consequences, and its relation to the literary elements of recent fiction, that I undertake this study. The five writers I have selected, writers who hold rather central positions in the present literary picture, reveal, despite their many differences, a far-reaching interest in the conflict their characters perceive between the personal and public, the religious and nonreligious sides of their lives.

Before turning to an analysis and interpretation of the works of these five writers and to a discussion of the form this conflict takes in each, we should look at the broader context in which these writers are working. A description is required here of the dominating literary characteristics of recent fiction and of the shape of the present religious situation. The most direct way of describing recent fiction is to detail the characteristics of its predominantly confessional form, while an equally direct analysis of the present religious situation must concern the nature and consequences of contemporary religious pluralism. The confessional form of fiction and the religiously pluralistic situation are parallel phenomena, but it would appear that one reason for the present interest in confessional fiction lies in the nature of problems raised for us by the pluralism of religious life.

Two characteristics of confessional fiction ought to be isolated. First, confessional fiction is a form that is centered around the narrator's or character's struggle with some significant problem in human life. Second, the world of a confessional fiction is a highly personal one, a world which has as its Atlas the word "I."

The two consequences of the pluralistic religious situation which ought to be isolated are these: a division between religious and nonreligious life and thought and a separation of personal or private matters from public ones. In other words, the pluralistic religious situation tends to create two realms, one for religious and for personal life and the other for life that is nonreligious and public. Before looking more closely at these consequences, let us examine the primary characteristics of the confessional form of fiction.

RECENT FICTION AND THE RELIGIOUS SITUATION

I

The first characteristic of confessional fiction, a deep concern for some significant problem in human life, constitutes the basis for the distinction Northrop Frye makes between the confession and three other forms of fiction: the novel, the romance, and the anatomy. Distinctions of this sort have been made by other critics, too, but they have been limited primarily to distinguishing the novel from the romance.[2] A critical consensus has now developed concerning the natures of these two forms of fiction.[3] The novel is generally seen as a type of fiction which, as one person describes it, concentrates on the characters' "inescapable involvement in society."[4] It is a form which is oriented toward the social, the public, and the ordinary aspects of human life. Consequently, this form tends to be governed by the "logical and the chronological" expressions and interests of human life. In contrast, the romance bears "a more literal relationship to the emotional nature of man."[5] As much as the novel tends toward the external world and toward order, the romance tends toward the internal world and toward the unexpected, the bizarre, and the gratuitous. Frye, while establishing this kind of contrast between the novel and the romance, goes on to distinguish two other forms of fiction, the anatomy and the confession. The type "anatomy" appears to include fiction which arises from an intellectual scheme, a scheme which is projected outwards and is presented as though it were an actual state of affairs. An anatomy, then, is a form of fiction which, like the novel, is oriented to an external world, but it is so only in appearance. Actually, the external world is created and controlled by categories arising from the implied author's interpretations of what the world really is, what it ought to be, or what it is almost certain to become. Robert

2. Cf. especially Richard Chase, *The American Novel and Its Tradition* (London: G. Bell and Sons, 1957).
3. Walter Allen, *Tradition and Dream* (London: Phoenix House, 1964), p. xiii.
4. Edwin Moseley, *Pseudonyms of Christ in the Modern Novel: Motifs and Methods* (Pittsburgh: University of Pittsburgh Press, 1961), p. 96.
5. Ibid., p. 97.

Scholes seems to have this form of fiction in mind when he calls attention to the mode which he terms "fabulation," intellectually or ethically controlled fantasy.[6]

Confession differs from the other forms of fiction in that the narrator is, according to Frye, concerned about a problem; he is engaged by some significant aspect of thought, whether in "religion, politics, or art."[7] Unlike the novel, which tries to dissolve all theory into social or personal relationships, unlike the anatomy, in which what is intellectual is expressed in the fiction as a set of determining ideas providing the scheme or framework for the story, and unlike the romance, which is more attentive to the emotional life of characters, confessional fiction is shaped by the narrator's own struggle with an important problem, a struggle which allows him to consider his experience worth telling about.

A second characteristic of confessional fiction, a more formal one, is that in it one rather than some other major element of fiction is of primary importance. Tone, the quality or manner of subjective presence, is the fictional element which is most central to this form. The other elements of fiction are atmosphere, plot, and character, and, while tone will be most central to the shape and power of a confessional fiction, these other elements will be present too. Atmosphere is that aspect of the characters' or narrator's situation which they or he cannot alter, which is given. Very often in recent fiction the atmosphere is inhospitable or even hostile to the well-being, desires, and expectations of the characters and narrator. Plot is the temporal synthesis of the story, a synthesis which gives a pattern to the events, the parts of which are organically related to one another. Usually the parts of the plot are three: the clarification of the situation of the principal character, the complication or aggravation of that situation, and its resolution. Character constitutes the primary image-making effect of the language of a fiction. To speak of the tone of a fiction is to describe, in distinction from these other elements, the stance the narrator assumes before what he is telling and his attitude toward his material.

6. Robert Scholes, *The Fabulators* (New York: Oxford University Press, 1967), pp. 11–14.
7. Northrop Frye, *Anatomy of Criticism: Four Essays* (New York: Atheneum, 1966), p. 308.

4

RECENT FICTION AND THE RELIGIOUS SITUATION

Since the narrator's presence is the most important element of fiction for the confessional form, use of the first person singular pronoun is common. "I" is the base of the fictional world created by a confession. This means that the struggle with some problem in "religion, politics, and art," the characteristic isolated by Frye, is not an impersonal struggle with an abstract idea from which personal interests have been expunged; the struggle is with a problem in which the narrator or principal character has a personal stake. A solution to that problem and his ability to say "I" with some understanding of what the word "I" means are intimately tied together.

Almost every study of recent fiction gives consideration to its preoccupation with personal identity, with, as I have put it, the question concerning the force and meaning of the word "I." Beginning in the forties, "Americans were trying to meet in literature the same dangers to the existence of man as man that Europeans were meeting in philosophy, and . . . Americans were reaching, more or less independent of Europeans, similar conclusions."[8] The preoccupation with the self in American fiction has been stimulated and fortified since the Second World War by the increasing influence of European writers, especially Sartre and Camus, on the American mind. In confessional fiction, attention is focused on the self as a center of authority and meaning which provides unity and significance for events, objects, and people standing otherwise in no significant relationship with one another. But it should also be said that at a time when the authority and meaning of the self are so commonly evoked, saying "I" in no relation to an all-inclusive and satisfying community or ideology is problematic. Consequently, the "I" constitutes not only the base from which confessional fiction arises, but also an object of quest for the sake of which the fiction is narrated.[9]

8. Chester E. Eisinger, *Fiction of the Forties* (Chicago: University of Chicago Press, 1967), p. 309. On this correspondence also consult Ihab Hassan, *Radical Innocence: The Contemporary American Novel* (Princeton: Princeton University Press, 1961), p. 9.

9. For a more complete study of the possibilities and problems in this preoccupation with the self in recent fiction, please see my essay, "Recent Fiction and Its Religious Implications," *Comparative Literature Studies* 3, no. 2 (1966), especially pp. 226–29. In addition, see the following studies:

5

INTRODUCTION

When we speak of confessional fiction either in terms of the characteristics mentioned by Frye or in terms of the narrator's position and opinions, we should remind ourselves, as has already been suggested, that the one who confesses—or the subjectivity which we meet in a work of fiction—is not to be identified as the author. We are dealing, rather, with what Wayne Booth calls the "implied author."[10] There always exists some distance between the implied or created author and the real author, since the implied author is the creation of the real author and resides, now, in the book. It is his attitudes which we are invited to share, "the chief value to which this implied author is committed, regardless of what party his creator belongs to in real life. . . ."[11] Critics have referred to personal presence or tone in fiction in many ways: "conceptual power" which puts to use the tools of style and sensibility (Wright Morris),[12] "a mode of vision" (Irving Howe),[13] or a sense of life (Arthur Mizener).[14] By whatever name, the quality or manner of the subjective presence will always be felt in a fiction, while in recent American fiction, with its commonly confessional nature, it will be a frequently dominant element.

To speak of fiction in terms of its elements is not necessarily to deny the integrity and primacy of fictional language. The so-called New Critics and, most recently and forcefully, David Lodge[15] have

---

Stanley R. Hopper, "The Problem of Moral Isolation in Contemporary Literature," in *Spiritual Problems in Contemporary Literature*, ed. S. R. Hopper (New York: Harper and Brothers, 1952), pp. 153–73; Leslie Fiedler, *An End to Innocence* (Boston: Beacon Press, 1955); Wright Morris, *The Territory Ahead* (New York: Harcourt, Brace and Co., 1957), especially pp. 230–31; R. W. B. Lewis, *The Picaresque Saint* (Philadelphia: J. B. Lippincott Co., 1959); and Nathan A. Scott, "Society and the Self in Recent American Literature," *Union Seminary Quarterly Review* 18 (May 1963) and *The Unquiet Vision: Mirrors of Man in Existentialism* (New York and Cleveland: World Publishing Co., 1969).

10. Wayne Booth, *The Rhetoric of Fiction* (Chicago: University of Chicago Press, 1961), p. 138.
11. Ibid., pp. 73–74.
12. Morris, *The Territory Ahead*, p. 229.
13. Irving Howe, *A World More Attractive: A View of Modern Literature and Politics* (New York: Horizon Press, 1963), p. x.
14. Arthur Mizener, *The Sense of Life in the Modern Novel* (Boston: Houghton Mifflin Co., 1964), p. 13.
15. David Lodge, *Language and Fiction: Essays in Criticism and Verbal Analysis of the English Novel* (New York: Columbia University Press, 1966).

made us aware of the fact that we cannot use the language of a poem or a fiction as an occasion to talk about something else, as though the language of a fiction constituted a window through which we could look at the author or at the people and events of the "real" world. To the same degree, we ought not to use the language of a fiction as an occasion to talk about literary-critical concepts. There are no plots or characters in a fiction; there are only the words of which the work is constituted. But it is possible to use such terms and not violate the integrity and primacy of literary language if we intend them as summaries and interpretations of the principal linguistic effects of a fictional work.

Finally, we should pause a moment to see that the relation of tone, the subjective presence, to the other elements of a fiction is an organic one. For example, plot becomes less important when tone increases—not because plot is being neglected by the author but because a temporal synthesis of the action wanes as the presence of subjectivity rises. This is true because tone tends to be static, somewhat fixed at the outset, while plot implies movement. If the quality or manner of the narrator's presence changes in the work, he has merged his voice with the plot, and plot has become more important than tone. Similarly, the flexibility and richness of the subjective presence are increasingly limited as atmosphere, that which the narrator and characters cannot alter, becomes more important. And, finally, when tone controls character, the characters are rendered not independently but in terms of the narrator's attitude toward them. It is inevitable, then, that in a confessional fiction, atmosphere, plot, and character, while present, are not of central importance. This organic relationship between tone and the other elements may be seen in some examples. Ken Kesey's *One Flew Over the Cuckoo's Nest* appears to be a work dominated by tone, since it is narrated in the first person by Chief Bromden. But the Chief allows the plot, of which Kesey's Samson-like McMurphy is the protagonist, to control the tone, and the Chief's own development and eventual cure become aspects of that plot. The relation of tone to atmosphere can be seen in Camus's *La Peste*. The heavy atmosphere may be thought to increase in intensity without reducing the tone. But the atmosphere is controlled by the subjective

presence and becomes personified by him or is used by him as a
kind of pressure principle applied to characters to reveal what they
actually are like. And the relation of tone to character can be seen
in John Knowles's *A Separate Peace*. The principal character is
shaped in terms of the narrator's attitudes toward him, attitudes
arising from the fact that Phineas brought Gene Forrester, the
narrator, to an early maturity.

II

Putting aside for the time being a consideration of the principal
characteristics of confessional fiction, we should turn now to look
at some of the effects for our society created by the religiously
pluralistic situation. The first of these effects is that religious life is
separated from what is nonreligious.

The pluralistic religious situation requires the construction in our
society of a common life which is nonreligious. This nonreligious
domain is an intentional construct of the society, one created in
order to allow Catholics, Protestants, and Jews to move about and
to do their work without encountering conflicting religious criteria
and appeals. This nonreligious construct exerts a unifying influence
on the society primarily in terms of daily work. Several sociologists
of religion have pointed out that religious norms and feelings enter
and affect this nonreligious realm through such things as national
celebrations, voting patterns, and censorship.[16] But such overlap-
pings or incursions are occasional and partial. American society
tends to be unified less by a language derived from religious ideas
and practices than by a language derived from the scientific, rational, and empirical perspectives and methods of daily work.

The situation of separation roughly conforms, then, to a separation between the day and the night life, between problem and mystery, between work and retreat. Given this perspective and method,

16. Cf., e.g., W. Lloyd Warner, *American Life: Dream and Reality* (Chi-
cago: University of Chicago Press, 1962), J. Milton Yinger, *Sociology
Looks at Religion* (New York: Macmillan Co., 1963), John Cogley, ed.,
Religion in America (Cleveland: World Publishing Co., 1958), and Robert
N. Bellah, "Civil Religion in America" in William G. McLoughlin and
Robert N. Bellah, eds., *Religion in America* (Boston: Beacon Press, 1968),
pp. 3–24.

it is difficult for people to address their activity in the public domain with norms and attitudes derived from their religion, and it is correspondingly difficult for people to derive from the public domain norms and attitudes for dealing with insoluble problems, such as undeserved pain, death, and pervasive evils.

We ought to see that the coincidence of the world of work with the nonreligious domain is not a fact which the dominant religions of the society resist with much passion. That is, a split between the religious-withdrawn and the nonreligious-engaged is encouraged not only by the public domain, which requires an atmosphere for work which is free from conflicting religious authorities, but also by Christianity and Judaism. These traditions are not marked by a strong desire to keep the world of work within the religious tent.

Judaism and Christianity tend to be suspicious of human invention and cultural achievement; the Bible often appears to tie the development of human culture to the development of human evil. In the primeval history in Genesis, for example, it is not the line favored by God that makes cultural advances; not Seth's line but Cain's produces cities, musical instruments, and metal tools. And it is not surprising that the God who rejected the city and the tower of Babel is also the one who chose Abraham. Abraham, for all his stature, was a seminomad, a man who lived off the land without planting, a man who, when drought struck, went to Egypt to live with people who knew how to work. It should not be surprising that the story of the degeneration of Lot, Abraham's nephew, should begin with Lot's choice of the fertile valleys and the cities of the plain, the first choice suggesting the move from the seminomadic to the agrarian and the second choice suggesting the move from the agrarian to the urban conditions. This rather normal move up the cultural ladder seems resisted at various points in the Bible, especially by the prophets, who often called Israel back from the cities and the farms to the wilderness, the seminomadic situation. The emphasis is no different in the New Testament. Jesus calls men away from their nets, and he is no friend of the cities. There are, in short, few, if any, cultural heroes in the Bible. Judaism and Christianity, then, seem not deeply committed to preventing the nonreligious domain from taking to itself the world of work.

Meanwhile, the nonreligious domain has developed a limited but consistent and rather adequate conceptual system to unify and promote its activities. Its language is derived from and tested by criteria of internal, logical, or imaginative consistence or of empirical verification. By implication it relegates to the religious-private realm whatever is gratuitous, unquestionably authoritative, and eternal.

The presence of this conceptual system alerts us to the second effect of a religiously pluralistic society, a loss of the personal in the world of work. The nonreligious domain is a public world unified by a conceptual system which, if it can be seen as epitomized in the work of one man, owes more to Descartes than to anyone else. It is a system based on the ruthless exclusion of the personal, a systematic skepticism which renders the "I" an eye measuring mathematically the relations to one another of phenomena in the objective world. Martin Buber, the most influential voice in a large supporting chorus of philosophers, theologians, and students of contemporary society, has alerted us to the loss of the personal which threatens human interaction, the loss of the personal in both the "I" and the "thou." Since it is the nonreligious, public world of work which unifies the society, the effects of this depersonalization are far-reaching, too deep, perhaps, to be overcome or balanced by a correspondingly significant and forceful participation by individuals in private religious communities in which the depth of human self-awareness and interaction can be nurtured and experienced.

III

Having described the characteristics of confessional fiction and the effects of a pluralistic religious situation, we may now be in a position to illuminate more clearly points at which these characteristics and effects appear to coincide. Remembering that the characteristics of confessional fiction are its emphasis on personal subjectivity, its interest in the meaning of "I," and its engagement with some significant problem, and remembering that the religious situation is marked by a separation between the religious and nonreligious and between the private and the public, we may be able to clarify some significant interrelationships.

The first characteristic of confessional fiction is that, while being written for the public, nonreligious world, it brings into that world the attitudes and struggles of the private life. As it brings private and internal life into the public domain, confessional fiction bridges the gap between the separated components, public and private. Of course, all fiction, literature, and art do this because they constitute the creations of private, individual imaginations. But confessional fiction by definition allows the presence of subjectivity to dominate, and the other elements, atmosphere, character, and plot, which may have more public overtones, are less important.

In addition, when the narrators of confessional fiction make clear that religion was or is an important aspect of their youthful or internal lives, religious attitudes and struggles are brought, with private memories and feelings, into the public domain. The fictions selected for this study are of that sort, and they play a particularly important role between the private and public or religious and nonreligious domains.

The subjective orientation of confessional fiction means that the narrator to a great degree withdraws himself from the structures and communities which are associated with both the religious and the nonreligious worlds. This puts him in an awkward position, since it implies a judgment on both worlds, a plague on both houses. But it is a gesture or pattern revealing great strength, too, since it implies a heroic individuality. It reveals a confidence in the stoutness of the self, and it rests on the assurance that the self, by itself, is important and that the reader will think so too. The plunge into subjectivity is a quest, then, and, although it may not be a quest for some graillike, redemptive object, the quest as a gesture draws attention to the potential for improvisation that resides in the self.

It should be no surprise, however, that both religious and non-religious readers should be somewhat impatient with the fascination for subjectivity evidenced by recent fiction and especially by its confessional form. On the one side objection can be raised because this move to the self can be seen as a withdrawal from the structures of society, because those structures are not wholly satisfying, into a dreamworld of illusion and half-remembered youth. Leslie

INTRODUCTION

Fiedler, for example, applying Freudian insights to his study of literary history in America, speaks convincingly about aspects of our literature which can be called simply immature and boyish.[17] We have only to think of the number of children and the fascination for childhood given to us by recent fiction to recognize a pervasive longing for youth, detachment, and innocence. In addition, objections can be raised from the other side, for when the self becomes primary in a fictional world all meaning and authority depend for their existence on the self's ability to fit them into its world. This makes the self the final arbiter over whatever shall be permitted existence or serious consideration, including religious doctrines, actions, or objects.[18] The self in that position may desire a religious view of life, but it is not able to find one, for, being in an authoritative position, it must provide that for which it looks. In the fiction we shall study, the self is often in a position of determining and passing judgment on the power of religion. In that position, the narrators and principal characters, securing their identities by refusing to solve their uncertainties with an answer that comes from without, stand in a deeply problematic relation to religion.

Turning to the characteristic of confessional fiction mentioned by Northrop Frye, struggle with a significant problem in human life, we shall see that this problem often arises from the separation of the language of religion from daily interests and needs.

In *Morte D'Urban* the form of the problem is the Church's conflict with human power within but especially outside of the Church. In *The Blood of the Lamb* the problem arises from the tension between belief in transcendent power and the experience of human suffering and loss. The problem in *The Centaur* is one of vocation, the lack of personally enriching daily work. *The Fixer* turns to the problem created by the failure of history to be religiously meaning-

17. Leslie Fiedler, *An End to Innocence* and *Love and Death in the American Novel* (New York: Criterion Books, Inc., 1960).
18. Cf., e.g., William Lynch, *Christ and Apollo* (New York: Sheed and Ward, 1960), p. 130, Edmund Fuller, *Man in Modern Fiction: Some Minority Opinions on Contemporary Writing* (New York: Random House, 1949), especially his charge that contemporary fiction teaches "belief in the reality of the self *alone*" (p. 160, my italics), and Stanley R. Hopper, "The Problem of Moral Isolation in Contemporary Literature."

ful, the experience of the death of God. And William Styron's controversial book, *The Confessions of Nat Turner*, is centered around the question of the relation of human revolution and violence to divine wrath and judgment. I have distorted the books by describing them in this hasty way, but I want only to indicate that in each book the problems, although individual and separable, are caused or aggravated by a common, underlying separation between the religious or private and the nonreligious or public domains.

It should not be surprising that critics speaking for both domains are at times impatient with this kind of fiction. Some readers have no interest in religious struggles and attitudes. More will fail to appreciate such matters when they are associated with a particular religious tradition or community as these are; not all will be interested in the Catholic attitudes of narrators and characters in the fiction of J. F. Powers, or in the Lutheranism of some of John Updike's people, or in the Dutch Reformed background of several of Peter De Vries's characters, or in the largely Jewish nature of Bernard Malamud's fictional world. On the other side, members of these religious communities may very likely be distressed with what happens to matters of religion when they are brought into the public domain, for what is of primary or authoritative importance for the life of a Catholic or Protestant or Jew will become secondary or a matter of opinion when these works make confessional life intelligible to a wide and pluralistic audience.[19] Despite a loss of interest on both sides, these fictions gain great stature by moving in the gap between the religious and nonreligious, the private and public realms, for they are cultural forms able to create a single whole out of what many readers experience as significant but separated parts.

Recent American fiction, including the works of the five writers we shall study later, stands, with its largely confessional nature, in a provocative middle position between the private and the public or the religious and the nonreligious realms, between the language of mystery and the language of problem-solving. It establishes in that position a middle ground or, as Frank Kermode would have it, an

19. For more on this point please see my essay, "Recent Fiction and the Christian Reader," *The Reformed Journal* 16, no. 7 (1966):17–19.

aevum[20] between the two domains. Geoffrey Hartman puts the matter nicely when he says:

> Human life, like a poetical figure, is an indeterminate middle between overspecified poles always threatening to collapse it. The poles may be birth and death, father and mother, love and judgment, heaven and earth, first things and last things. Art narrates that middle region and charts it like a purgatory. . . .[21]

The middle region which we shall explore lies somewhere between the "overspecified poles" of the religious and the nonreligious.

In each chapter, one major work of each writer will be analyzed and interpreted in terms of its dominant literary elements and in terms of the problem with which the narrator or principal character is struggling. Further, we shall see that the problem in each case is solved not in rational terms but through the narrator's or character's experience of a newly clarified and identified force and significance to his use of the word "I." After that, the particular fiction will be placed in relation to the other major fictional works of the author, and the extent to which his preoccupation may be reflected by other fiction in this period will be suggested. Each chapter will end with a discussion of the particular religious matter explored by each writer, the issues of authority, transcendent power, vocation, the death of God, and revolution. These discussions will hopefully reveal how human experiences may at one time have held religious meaning and will suggest why those meanings have lost their public force. And finally, in the Conclusion, we shall return to the underlying problem which has already been outlined and which these works appear to share, the separation of religious from nonreligious understandings. Predictably, I shall at the end want to suggest for this underlying problem a somewhat personal solution.

20. Frank Kermode, *The Sense of an Ending* (New York: Oxford University Press, 1967), pp. 70–71.
21. Geoffrey H. Hartman, *Beyond Formalism: Literary Essays 1958–1970* (New Haven: Yale University Press, 1970), p. 348.

1

Morte D'Urban and the Presence of Clergy

Clergymen in recent fiction are generally unattractive, and those found in the works assembled for this study are no exceptions. This depiction of uncomely clergy does not necessarily arise from an attitude of antiprofessionalism; while the clergy in these five works look weak, foolish, or destructive, the physicians, especially in De Vries's fiction and in Updike's, are resources of wisdom and strength. De Vries goes out of his way to satirize Protestant ministers, especially, of course, in *The Mackerel Plaza*; but while the ministers in *The Blood of the Lamb* look, if anything, worse than the Reverend Mackerel, the narrator has a great respect for members of the medical profession. In *The Centaur*, Dr. Appleton is a resource for both Peter and his father, but the Reverend March is portrayed as more interested in sex than in the religious questions George asks him, a preference, incidentally, that several of Updike's other clergymen would share, especially the Episcopal priest Jack Eccles in *Rabbit, Run* who likes to spend his time talking with young people about how far they can go and still love Jesus. Little attention need be drawn to the priestly portraits in *The Fixer*, since the Orthodox clergy is so clearly depicted in its demonic, anti-Semitic role. And the white clergy in *The Confessions of Nat Turner* are terribly unattractive men. To the degree that *Morte D'Urban* is an exposure of the clergy's weaknesses or folly, then, it is consistent with the other works to be considered here.

One reason for anticlericalism appears to be the desire of these writers to heap on one representative all the unfortunate associations with religion they can expect their readers to make and, at the same time, to release from disdain the means or representative of grace or wisdom which these writers may want to bring forward in the rejected clergy's stead. In De Vries's fiction, for example, the narrators and protagonists are repeatedly engaged with explicitly religious matters, but clergymen are not helpful in those engagements. This is also true of several of Updike's ministers, as it is, for example, in the story "Pigeon Feathers" where David gets no help from his pastor in his search for an answer to dying, but finds his answer instead in the beauty of pigeon feathers. Malamud is not dismissing spiritual resources in his treatment of Orthodox clergy any more than he is dismissing political possibilities by his treatment of the Tsar. Finally, Nat Turner's role as a clergyman is to bring into his world a dimension of religious reality which the white clergy have obscured, namely, the wrath of God against the sins of slavery. In all these cases clergymen are treated harshly so that the power or truth which they should but do not give can be received by the character through a form which, in contrast to rejected clergy, looks attractive.

This attack on false or foolish spiritual representatives as a way of getting behind them to more convincing or significant spiritual resources is a move, I believe, quite central to J. F. Powers's award-winning book, *Morte D'Urban*. It is more than a sardonic, Bergsonian laugh at all or at one kind of Catholic clergy. Rather than constituting an attack on the Church or clergy, Powers's pleasingly comic fiction secures a modest but indispensable place for spiritual resources in American life by killing off with gentle stabs an outrageous instance of false clerical identity.

I

Perhaps the structural device is too subtle to be convincing, but *Morte D'Urban* appears to be a confession of sin. If so, it is not Powers's exposure of the clergy but Father Urban's description of his own pride and folly, a way of life which has, fortunately, died off or been killed. The italicized preface keeps us from standing outside of the Church or apart from Father Urban laughing at one or both of them. It puts us in the pew and in Father Urban's confidence. In the preface Urban is speaking, and he exhorts us to laugh—but not at the Father Provincial, "who, of course, is accountable to Someone Else"; we are exhorted, finally, to laugh at the way that "Someone Else" brings important results from small occasions. The important result for the narration is the slow death of Father Urban's folly and pride through the small occasions of mishaps, failures, and abuse. The work, then, is a confession of sin and a celebration of (how should it be put?) Someone's grace, a work in which tone, the presence of subjectivity, however hidden, is of primary importance.

Before looking at the sins which are confessed or exposed in the narration, we ought to notice the other characteristic of confessional fiction to which Northrop Frye alerted us, the struggle with some significant problem. The problem here is the relation of the Church to worldly power, a problem both internal to the Church—the relation of the Church's spirit or mission to its specific forms—and external to it—the Church's relation to influential but nonreligious people and organizations. Giving depth to this problem is the recurring Arthurian motif, for, as we shall see later on, this problem lies deep in Christian history. Consequently, Malory and the medieval period stand behind the problem as medieval piety stands behind the confession of sin in the figure of St. Bernard and in the form of his *De Gradibus Humilitatis.*

Father Urban has habits unbecoming to a priest. When he travels, which is every chance he gets, he goes first-class on money kept from gifts to him, a practice built on the "spirit" rather than on the "letter" of the law. He is, in his own view, an exceptional case, and he would be head of his Order "if the members of the Order had only known that by electing him Provincial they would not be losing him in the field."[1] Attesting to his exceptional abilities is his sense of successfully handling or manipulating occasions, individuals, and crowds. He is not far, in other words, from what Sally Hammond calls him later on, an "operator," a person who is

1. J. F. Powers, *Morte D'Urban* (Garden City: Doubleday and Co., Inc., 1962), p. 26.

pleasant to other people not because he likes them or is really interested in them but because he manipulates them to his own or, as he often insists, the Order's benefit.

In addition, Father Urban is not much of a worshiping priest. He admits that he spends little time in prayer or before the Sacrament, excusing himself on the basis of his frequent travel. This attitude arises from an antipathy he had even as a boy toward all in Catholic rituals which offended the respectable, intellectual Protestants of his southern Illinois hometown.

The third questionable habit of Father Urban is his competitive spirit. This he gets from the redeemer figure of his youth, Father Placidus, who showed the boy another image of the clergy. A man for whom athletics held almost as much value as religion and for whom high living seems to have been the highest good, Father Placidus provides a motto for Urban and for the book's comically medieval emblem, *"Be A Winner."* Since his opponents within the Order lack Urban's talents, he considers himself to be uncontestedly the Order's star performer. His strength is only tested by clergy outside of the Order, as in the struggle with Signor Renton over the question of building a new church at St. Monica's and in the golfing match with the Bishop's team. The only advantage the less gifted members of the Order have over him is their authoritative positions, and Father Urban's greatest hardship in life is having to obey people, such as the Provincial and Wilf, the rector of St. Clement's Hill, who are less gifted than he. Their unenlightened attitudes form the major obstacle Urban must vault on his way to the goal of raising the Order's tone.

The need to obey inferior people leads to the final questionable attitude found in Urban, his frequent resentment. He resents being sent from Chicago to the wilds of Minnesota, and he resents having to work there as a common laborer under Wilf. He sustains himself in these periods by maintaining "a secret ascendancy over the life around him"[2] and by working "in a quiet rage."[3]

The work's central problem, the Church's relation to nonreligious structures and powers, is one which Father Urban, during most of

2. Ibid., p. 86.
3. Ibid., p. 126.

the account, thinks he has adequately solved. He wants the structure of the Church to take on a more attractive form, attractive, that is, to people of the "better" sort, people of wealth and prestige. Quite consistent with this is his opinion that the Church ought to become cordial with people and organizations that make a difference in the world, regardless of their Christian or non-Christian identity.

Urban's association with Billy is a confirmation and test of his approach, and for a period of time he is convinced that since Billy Cosgrove can or has pulled the Order from obscurity and weakness to fame and influence, Urban's program is a winning strategy. With a new location on Chicago's North Side and the gifts received at Deusterhaus, especially the golf course, the Order has been put on the map. Convinced that his relationship with Billy is a fruitful one, he attempts to establish similar relationships with other people, especially with Mrs. Thwaites, the donor of the Deusterhaus buildings.

Urban feels that his program is consistent with great moments in the Church's history. He compares himself favorably with those of former centuries who created fortunate alliances with worldly power. Surely he has reservations about Billy's manner, but "some of the most powerful figures in history had been spoiled children like Billy, but humble monks had brought them to their knees and turned their bloody hands to the service of God."[4] As he rides with Mrs. Thwaites on the lake he has a "vision of life in late medieval times."[5] When things do not go well in his program of reconciliation, he thinks of himself as linked to that band of martyrs who suffered for the Church by hobnobbing with kings, a band he would like to commemorate with a book: "Lambs Who Lay Down with Lions and Lived."[6]

Urban's desire to unify Church and world results in an insensitivity to instances of conflict between the two. He is, naturally, uninterested in Wilf's campaign to put Christ back into Christmas, since the issue is a rather insignificant and crotchety one. However,

4. Ibid., pp. 23–24.
5. Ibid., p. 257.
6. Ibid., p. 287.

in his speech he fails to recognize the deeper issue of materialism, and he unqualifiedly endorses merchant attitudes as acceptable to God. Similarly, Urban was widely quoted in the Catholic press for his early and uncritical acceptance of television. And in his conversations with the Beans and Zimmerman about economic and political questions he is unable to clarify real areas of strife beneath the rather crude expression of this strife in Zimmerman's letters or in the *Drover*.

Toward the end of the account, however, Father Urban has increasing difficulties with Billy and with the Thwaites family, and his solution to the problem of the Church's relation to worldly power finally crumbles. With these recurring setbacks, a question is also lodged about Urban's identity, since his answer and his manner are so closely linked. The fall of his solution and the rise of his humility, consequently, coincide.

The episodes in which Urban's confidence and solutions are exposed, tested, and dismantled are divided into three sections: those presenting Urban's confinement to St. Clement's Hill, chapters one through five; those depicting his release and rise, chapters six through ten; and those revealing his conflicts, failures, and defeats, chapters eleven through fifteen. Although he experiences setbacks in all sections, only those in the last seriously threaten his identity as an exceptional man.

The major setback of the first part, of course, is his consignment to Deusterhaus, an insult coming to him at the height of his success with Billy Cosgrove. Consequently, he sees the consignment as a colossal instance of the Provincial's lack of good sense. There is little in Deusterhaus worthy of his presence, and his exile is aggravated by the work he is asked to do, by the cold, and by the incompetence of those with whom he lives.

The setback of the second part is Urban's inability to secure St. Monica's parish for himself. He works hard there, apparently in order to advance himself. He favors the erection of a new edifice, steps up church activities, moves at a frantic pace, and caps his stay with a week of brilliant preaching. Urban is very pleased with his work at St. Monica's, and he expects that the fortunate death of Phil will create a natural place for him there. He is thrown for an unexpected loss, then, when the Bishop suggests that he minister to a church not of St. Monica's sort but to three Indian missions in the north.

The setbacks of the final part are the most devastating. For a man who has turned St. Clement's Hill into a successful operation, he deserves more than he gets at the hands of Zimmerman and the parish of which Zimmerman is the wealthiest member. Urban suffers again at the end of his contest with the Bishop's team on the golf course; he is struck on the head, an injury from which he never fully recovers. Further, Urban's alliance with Billy crumbles. On the fishing trip, Urban realizes how he has failed to recognize the "cruel streak" in Billy, his intimidation of others, his self-centeredness and insensitivity. He learns, for example, that Billy bought the Order's new address because he wanted to oust a record dealer who had been discourteous to him. Billy is a powerful man whose generosity is only a partially disguised self-interest. Consequently, Urban is already suspicious of Billy when Billy grossly oversteps proprieties by trying to drown a deer, an act which recalls the picture Brother Harold painted representing the Church as a deer drinking. Rather than let Billy twist or drown the "Church," Urban dunks him, and their relationship ends. Finally, Urban is humiliated in his associations with the Thwaites family. Sally tells him that he is an "operator—a trained operator . . . and an operator in your heart—and I don't think you have a friend in the world."[7] Smarting from this attack on his clerical identity, Urban, in the silence that follows, imagines himself to be a highly successful executive with a plush office, attractive, loyal secretaries, meetings with dignitaries, and experiences with many women. The temptation to actualize this erotic dream comes when Sally disrobes for a swim; when Urban refuses to join her, she rides off in the boat. Bereft of the means of transportation the world has always provided him, Urban makes his way back to the Hill on his own, a wet, humiliated man.

The spunk is gone from Urban. He neglects his contacts, gives up golf, and becomes ill. A literary parallel to Urban's experiences is offered by Father John's interest in Malory. Sir Lancelot is a

7. Ibid., p. 301.

failure and a sinner, and, although producing Galahad, his exploits in the world cause the fall of the Order of the Round Table. Dying to the world, Lancelot takes orders. Just so, Urban becomes a Provincial who is removed from the world. He is, to everyone's surprise, a wholly changed man; he allows the Order to suffer losses, and he travels no more, sees few people, and thinks of the Hill as his home.

The significance of Urban's confession, its acknowledgment of sin and its description of his ill-fated solution to the Church-world problem, is heightened by Powers's use of two sets of medieval material, Sir Thomas Malory's saga of Arthur and his knights and the writings of St. Bernard of Clairvaux, upon which, as Powers in a prefatory note points out, the vow-renewing ceremony is based. The influence of these works on the novel is quite crucial and clarifies the fact that Powers is interested in more than the exposure of one priest's folly. He is interested, rather, in bringing into focus a recurring problem and error in the Church.

The problem, the relation of the Church to worldly power, is heightened by reference to the Arthurian saga because the Order of Arthur was one unifying the spiritual and the secular, Church and state, a unity not finally realized in the particular Order Malory depicts but one that was always its goal. Malory stands between the times as a writer looking back on the partial realization of this ideal and looking forward to its future reestablishment.[8] Father Urban's Church also stands between the times, laboring with imperfect relations to the world, laboring even with antipathy between the two, but looking back and forward to peace and union. Arthur's Order, introduced at Pentecost, is an eschatological one, always an anticipated reality, and it is by this "not yet" that Urban is caught. Urban is a priestly-knight of the Order of St. Clement (the refectory has two tables and the clergy sit at the round one), and he works toward, or thinks he has attained, the eschatological "Now". of union between sacred and secular.

Father Urban's quixotic embodiment of an eschatological "Now" reveals a sense of uniqueness which he has of himself that Mrs.

8. Cf. Edmund Reiss, *Sir Thomas Malory* (New York: Twayne Publishers, Inc., 1966), pp. 38–42.

Thwaites's daughter only touches when she accuses Urban of having no friends. He has no friends because he feels, without seeming to recognize the extent of his megalomania, isolated as one of his kind healing the deep rift between clergy and laity and the Church and the non-Church. In fact, he is himself an embodiment of this new, eschatological union.

By his confidence in worldly wisdom, his skill in defeating his opponents, and his charm tempered by restraint in dealing with women, Urban has neglected the central virtues. He has substituted self-confidence for faith, realization of the new order within himself for hope, and manipulation and competition for charity. The result is an excessive pride, and Urban, by undertaking single-handedly the actualization of a new union has lost his place both in the Church and in the world. He is dissociated from Billy and the Thwaites, and he is resentful toward religious authority. When he realizes his position, Father Urban seems to recognize that his calling to orders was not a calling to pull the Order up to a tone set by worldly success but a calling to give himself to be a re-creation by the Order for an election to holiness.

The extent of Urban's faultiness is clarified by Powers's reference to St. Bernard. The Latin ceremony at the end is an improvisation on a Benedictine ceremony of this type constructed of quotations quite central to St. Bernard's *De Gradibus Humilitatis*. The reference to the three stages of truth is taken from a general discussion by St. Bernard of this matter in the opening pages of the tract. But the heart of the ceremony, from the "*Putas, primo homini . . .*" through "*Ad tertium puritas rapit,*"[9] is taken, with slight modification, from Bernard's discussion of the third degree of truth. And the final section on prayer, beginning with "*Et si contigerit . . . ,*"[10] is taken from the conclusion of Bernard's discussion of the degrees of pride, specifically his discussion of the question whether or not prayers can be offered for those who have descended the steps of pride to the depths of freedom to sin and contempt for God.[11] The

9. Powers, *Morte D'Urban,* pp. 327–29. .
10. Ibid., pp. 329–30.
11. Bernard of Clairvaux, *De Gradibus Humilitatis et Superbiae,* ed. Barton R. V. Mills, Cambridge Patristic Texts (Cambridge: Cambridge University Press, 1926), pp. 102–3 and p. 154.

treatise on humility and pride is based, in its first part, on the twelve degrees of humility which are enumerated in the seventh chapter of St. Benedict's "Rule." The discussion of pride in terms of twelve corresponding degrees is Bernard's invention.

The path to truth begins with humility, and humility is a painfully won recognition, discovered by self-scrutiny, of personal unworthiness. The effect of this scrutiny is that one sees himself to be no better than others. In addition, a man may conclude that his wretched condition is true of mankind in general. Once this sense of community arises the second course toward truth is enforced, love or compassion toward others. When a man can say in ecstasy that all men are liars, he gains a sense of community and loses a sense of uniqueness. Further, having suffered this painful realization, he has learned to sympathize with others. The final course of truth is full vision, given in and with purity. Bernard finds this threefold path no simple coincidence, since the Trinity can be discussed in these terms. Before the Son a man is a learner; in the Comforter men are friends; under the Father men become sons.

Beginning with curiosity, a state in which a man is more concerned about the positions of others relative to himself and more concerned with what others think of him than he is about the painful matter of self-scrutiny, Bernard traces twelve steps of pride. Probably working from his experiences with fellow monks, he describes men who are without humility and truth. One monk tries to do more than others so that his superiority may be apparent. He is not as interested in a better life as he is in surpassing others. If he does not do something himself, he concludes it has not been properly done. He is critical of his superiors. If he does not receive honors, he concludes that his superiors are mistaken or jealous of him. He is contemptuous of lowly duties, and even in acts of worship he tries to outdo others. Soon, he feels that his extraordinary character allows him to sin, and then, so impressed with himself is he, he finally is as contemptuous of God as he is of his superiors.

The culminating position in which the ceremony stands makes it the narrow passage through which Father Urban, as he renews his vows, passes. In relation to St. Bernard's prescription for the life of truth, then, Urban, far from presenting a comical caricature, confesses his false sense of the unity of Church and non-Church and his almost completed descent to Hell. The fact that he has no friends, that he considers himself uniquely singled out, that he constantly views himself in relation to others in the Order, that he is such a talker, that he indulges in merriment, that he obeys the letter of his superiors' orders but resents them in spirit, and that he even enters a state of disdain for the authority of Christ incarnate in the Church and the Order, reveal him as an enemy of Christ. Urban presents himself, then, as the opposite of what a servant of Christ is or should be. Consequently, the ceremony appears as not one of renewing but of taking vows, and Urban really begins his religious life, as did Lancelot, when he dies to the world.

In retreat from the problem of the Church's relation to the world, a new Urban, apparently, is in the process of being born, a man given to self-scrutiny and humility. The mark of humility would be the refusal to talk about one's spiritual struggle. This would account for the fact that during the dirge nothing is said of the scrutiny and the writing of this book. Consequently Powers is not in this book writing about the sins of others, an activity St. Bernard describes as curiosity. This is Urban's own confession, and it is consistent with spiritual principles set forth by St. Bernard.

The means by which Urban comes to realize the folly and evil of his sense of uniqueness and his attempt at solving in his own person the problem of the Church's relation to the world is not clear. It seems that Urban suddenly realizes that he is firmly footed on neither the Church nor the world but is suspended above the dark abyss of their separation. The profundity of that separation, of the problem, teaches him the first course in truth, his own ignorance, sinfulness, and folly. It teaches him humility.

Despite his sin, Urban can, at the end, be easily forgiven, perhaps not because pride is a light thing, but because of the problem. The agony of tragic separation, the rift between the Church and the world, an agony aggravated by the memory or the hope of their union, can easily send a man in quest of an answer. It is a problem with such dimensions that all other problems can seem neutralized in contrast, and one can be tempted to neglect the worthiness of means if the end, a solution to it, can, at least partially, be reached.

Urban is not as spared as others from awareness that what is most important in the world of the non-Church is often the most distant from the Church. One who suffers that problem can easily be forgiven false attempts at its solution.

II

The priestly portrait that Powers gives us in *Morte D'Urban* is not accidental to his work as a writer of fiction, and he puts before us, with his preoccupation with priests, problems in religious life which are significant for both American fiction and religion. Clergymen appear in recent fiction almost as often as they do in Powers's work, and one can easily list writers, in addition to those brought together for this study, who include clergy in their casts: James Agee, Frederick Buechner, John Knowles, Isaac Singer, Flannery O'Connor, and many more. This suggests that for American writers priestly attendance to a sacred presence is considered to be significant both for the contemporary American world and for the life of their art.

When a writer includes a clergyman in his cast of characters, questions of his religious authority arise for both the other characters and the reader. Answering these questions calls for a particularly subtle critical act. The position or words of a clergyman cannot be taken simply as one person's point of view, since, if nothing else, the clergyman represents the structure with which he is identified. By using clergy, a writer subjects his art to such questioning, and the answers may be widely different. Even Powers, who uses priests often and who is himself Catholic, divides opinion. Evelyn Waugh contends that Powers is a writer whose "whole art is everywhere infused and directed by his Faith,"[12] but Peter De Vries insists that Powers uses priests in order to present not clerical attitudes but human ones in a pointed way. His priests, De Vries says, are not members "merely of the Church, but of that much older community, the human race," and his view of man "is

12. Cited by Peter De Vries in J. F. Powers, *Lions, Harts, Leaping Does and Other Stories,* with an introduction by Peter De Vries (New York: Time Incorporated, 1963), p. xv.

everywhere thoroughly imbued with his skepticism."[13] The question, then, is this: Can the use of priests bring forward something both unique or authoritative and, at the same time, very human and common? I think answers to this question derived from Powers's fiction and the role of clergy in religious life will help us to see the potential which resides in the fictional use of priests.

A number of Powers's stories, found particularly in *Prince of Darkness and Other Stories*[14] (1948), are not concerned with priests and the Church, and it is interesting to note that these stories are attentive to conflict in American life. As with Malamud and Styron, Powers is especially fascinated by racial or ethnic tension in America. Tension, combat, and violence are more constant in his work than priests, and, I would suggest, Powers's interest in priests is determined greatly by his sensitivity to divisions and hostilities within American society.

"The Trouble," "The Eye," and "He Don't Plant Cotton" all depict racial tensions. The first, narrated by a young Negro boy, presents a moment of black-white violence. The separation between the two groups and two individuals is clearly given, but, through the death of the black man's wife, the conflict between the individuals is transcended. In the second, racism is so destructive a force that Clyde Bullen cannot defend an innocent black man against the unfounded charge of rape. And in the third story, white harassment of blacks is depicted in a rather unspectacular but not less demonic form, as the members of a black band find it increasingly difficult to create nice musical moments in the company of oppressive white patrons.

In another set of three stories, "Jamesie," "Renner," and "The Old-Bird, A Love Story," the violent or disappointing character of American life is also rendered, although not in terms of racial strife. Jamesie is deeply disappointed when the only figure of value in his otherwise tasteless world, a baseball player named Lefty, turns out to be a fraud, and Jamesie is left with a world as crude and friendless as is his motherless home. Renner, an immigrant, has

13. Ibid.
14. J. F. Powers, *Prince of Darkness and Other Stories* (New York: Doubleday and Co., Inc., 1948).

been made sensitive to subtle forms of violence by his European experiences. He relates how he defended at work a young girl intimidated by "Pressure From Above," and in the German restaurant where he is relating his experiences he comes to the defense of a Jew. Renner sees, as Powers seems to, little struggles and conflicts as symptomatic of major moral and spiritual battles and diseases. We find this interest also in the third story of this kind, in which an elderly man is forced to take a temporary, intimidating job in a factory shipping room. Humiliated and fatigued by his job, the man returns home in the evening to watch with his wife the darkness and the snow outside their window.

The isolated moments of peace and reconciliation in Powers's fiction are realized against a background of an America that is deeply troubled and disappointing. It is important to an understanding of Powers's priestly stories to keep this fact in mind.

The conflicts and disappointments in the clerical stories are little ones, but they are no less deeply felt. In "The Valiant Woman" Father Firman has doubts about his vocation, since he is given, instead of major sufferings, the nasty, enervating burdens of domestic life. He is a priest caught in, of all things, domestic tension with his housekeeper. The conflict is not more major in "The Forks," perhaps, but in the attitudes of the Monsignor and the curate we have more than a generation gap or a personality clash; we have conflicting understandings of the nature of the Church, the one carrying to an extreme St. Paul's tactic of becoming all things to all men in order to win some for Christ, and the other carrying the prophetic antagonism toward the ways of the world to a captious conclusion. Although Father Eudex is a more attractive character than the Monsignor, we ought not to think that Powers has resolved the tension between these two minds in the church. Finally, conflict in the Church is rendered in "The Lord's Day," and it is caused by an evil priest under whom the twelve valiant sisters suffer. Whether caused by little things, by differing vocational understandings, or by evil attitudes, conflicts in the Church are just as common and deeply felt as the tensions and struggles in the surrounding society.

Conflict also can arise within the life of a single priest, between what he knows he is called to be and what he actually is. Father

Burner has this problem without wholly realizing it in the title story from his collection. The prayer he has posted on his walls puts the matter well: "Remember, O most compassionate God, that they [priests] are but weak and frail human beings."[15] Father Burner, by revealing a greater interest in his own advancement than in the spiritual well-being of a parishioner, is still only on his way to becoming a priest. Internal struggle is also central to "Lions, Harts, Leaping Does," in which Father Didymus is both a priest and a weak, doubting man. Having been given no great trials, having experienced no great fruits on his work, tormented by the trite lives of parishioners, Didymus doubts his vocation and is almost thrown from disappointment to despair. Comparing himself to a canary, he feels "caged, stunted in his apostolate,"[16] seeking crumbs. The peace he finally achieves comes from without, from the snow falling and from the saintly presence of Brother Titus.

Conflicting attitudes found in the clergy are also present in the nonclerical stories of *The Presence of Grace*[17] (1956). Ethnic distinctiveness causes the Davicci family in "Blue Island" anxiety about their acceptability in a Swedish Protestant neighborhood, and this anxiety forces them into awkward and foolish moves. Their position parallels the more religious or clerical anxiety concerning social acceptability found in the other stories. And the two ladies of "The Poor Thing" express by their conflicting attitudes, the one morbid and excessively disciplined, the other casual and buoyant, differing outlooks found among Powers's priests. And in "The Devil Was the Joker" we find a young man with ideals about the Church's sacrificial role and its universality conflicting with the worldly attitudes of an older man, whose buying and selling, wheeling and dealing approach is untempered by ideals. The two extremes again expose a tension in ordinary life and in the Church, and they find their clerical parallel in "The Forks."

Two of the stories which emphasize the presence of grace in this collection, "Defection of A Favorite" and "Death of A Favorite," are narrated by an unlikely Christ-like figure, the rectory cat. At

15. Ibid., pp. 242–43.
16. Ibid., p. 67.
17. J. F. Powers, *The Presence of Grace* (New York: Atheneum, 1956).

one point the cat becomes a sacrificial substitute for its master, when antipathy of a priest toward the cat's master is expressed in hostility toward the cat. At another point, Fritz the cat confers authority on the rightful priest and teaches humility and obedience to another. The cat witnesses and participates in the struggles and reconciliation of rectory life; he stays throughout the crisis, suggesting that the presence of grace is not destroyed by rectory troubles. Grace is also present in the title story; the pastor is enabled to handle a crisis caused in the Church by his co-worker's lack of wisdom.

"Keystone," Powers's novella of 1963, gives, with *Morte D'Urban*, his fullest view of the problems in clerical life that threaten the presence of grace. The principal character, a bishop, is bound to the facts of his time. Trying to be relevant to his time, he is not relevant to all times; his championing of F. D. R. makes him a curiosity in the fifties. He and the new Chancellor are priests for the hour and not forever. Primarily, they have no tools to work with the current problem of prosperity, and the Church falls into the trap of high living. As it becomes a major business enterprise, the Church's spiritual, eternal nature is lost, and the Bishop feels this loss primarily in the erosion of his authority. The reader feels more fully than the Bishop that the Church in the world has become an ornamental nonnecessity. Rather than awakening to this fact, the Bishop at the end fears that his authority is threatened by the central position of the Chancellor.

Perhaps "Keystone" is Powers's most forceful exposure of the Church almost given over to the prince of darkness because of the conflicts, weaknesses, and destructive attitudes of its clergy. Certainly the exposure is gentle and subtle. Powers reveals an appreciation for the Church in its predicament because he has a feeling for the Church as a body suffering in exaggeration struggles and disappointments which are felt in the surrounding society. The implied point is of an *a fortiori* nature: if conflict is found in the society how much more can we expect it to be found in the Church; if the society is threatened by evil and destruction, how much more threatened is the Church; if, despite conflict, reconciliation and wisdom can be gained in the world, how much more possible are they in the Church. The Church and its clergy, with all that besets and rewards them, epitomize what distresses and heartens Powers in the society. The Church has in his fiction this natural authority: epitomizing what is found to be true of society.

On the other hand we ought not to forget that for Powers, or, at least, for his clergy, the Church does not simply bring to focus the powers of evil and reconciliation found more generally in the world. The Church has an authority also as an expression of that victory over evil and that reconciliation of men which has its origin and goal in something more than human. The experiences of Powers's clerics are enlarged not only by their parallels in the society but by their parallels to the fundamental struggle between the presence of grace and the prince of darkness. Endemic to these stories, then, is an estimation of the Church as the suffering presence of God in the world. For Powers's priests, God is not first of all everywhere or anywhere; he is first of all here in a specific form, the Church. This means that tensions within the Church and between the Church and the world expose the problematic character of man's relation to God.

The religiously authoritative character of the Church is not mitigated by the weakness of the clergy. In fact, while concealing the authority of the Church by these weaknesses, the clergy also expose that authority, for the authority has its source not in their personal strengths but in a power that lies beyond them. As St. Paul put it to the Corinthian Church: "God chose what is foolish in the world to shame the wise, God chose what is weak in the world to shame the strong, God chose what is low and despised in the world, even things that are not, to bring to nothing things that are, so that no human being might boast in the presence of God." Grace is, consequently, clarified as well as obscured by the weakness of its form.

The problem which gives rise to Powers's fiction is the problem of tension and division, division between groups of people in the society, between kinds of people in the Church, and between people within the Church and outside of it. Despite tensions and conflicts, and at times because of them, moments of reconciliation appear. The clerical fiction epitomizes this general problem and the moments of grace by a concentration within a specific structure of those problems and possibilities which are experienced in the society and by an identification of that structure as the scene of ultimate struggle and peace.

III

It may appear that Powers's interest in and use of the clergy is stimulated by a distinctively Catholic orientation. But the role of the priests in his fiction is one shared by Jewish and Protestant clergy, since an emphasis on the structure of grace is not exclusive to Catholicism.

Christians and Jews are agreed on the understanding that God takes on a specific form in the world of men. They have differed on the question of what that form is. Hebrews differed among themselves in the Old Testament on the question of whether or not that form was the city, dynasty, and cult of David. The North and the South were deeply divided on that question, as deeply divided as were Jews and Christians later over the question of whether or not in and through the person of Jesus a new form was established. Hebrews were also divided somewhat on the question of the relative authority of the wilderness experience and of the later developments in Hebrew life, the shrines and dynasties. This difference accounted greatly for the repeated clash between prophets and kings or priests, as with Elijah and Ahab. This tension was carried over into Christianity, and it is to be seen in the differing emphases on law in the New Testament. More recently, this tension gave rise to the Catholic-Protestant split, the one with its priestly and the other with its prophetic emphases. Paul Tillich identified this tension as one between "the Protestant principle" and "the Catholic substance" in religion.

> The Protestant principle (which is a manifestation of the prophetic Spirit) is not restricted to the churches of the Reformation or any other church; it transcends every particular church, being an expression of the Spiritual community. It has been betrayed by every church, including the churches of the Reformation, but is also effective in every church as the power which prevents profanation and demonization from destroying the Christian churches completely. It alone is not enough; it needs the "Catholic substance," the con-

crete embodiment of the Spiritual Presence; but it is the criterion of the demonization (and profanization) of such embodiment. It is the expression of the victory of the Spirit over religion.[18]

Of course, Tillich's emphasis is on the "Protestant principle," since he is highly prophetic and even mystical in the direction of his religious understandings, but he puts the matter well, seeing this tension as not one between religions but as one within all vital religion.

The "Catholic substance," the sense of God's presence in the world, then, is not a Catholic phenomenon; it is found in Judaism and Protestantism as well. This means that some moment or structure in the human world is considered to be of unique importance as the form of God's presence. However, Catholics have been particularly sensitive to this aspect of religious life, and they seem to feel more deeply than Protestants both the need of, and the problems in, identifying a structure with the presence of God. In order to treat this aspect of their life, Catholic theologians such as Romano Guardini, Josef Ratzinger, Karl Rahner, and Hans Küng have employed less static images to clarify the nature of the Church. In addition, they have emphasized the painfully disappointing character of the Church, its weaknesses, follies, and sins. Finally, they take very seriously the problem of the Church's relation to people and structures which stand in no conscious relation to Christianity.[19]

Powers has exposed with his fictions, then, a problem that is central to religious life, and he has used it to illuminate both the sufferings of American society and the suffering presence of God in the world. Under the surfaces of his fictions, which are often smooth, pleasant, and comical, lie these deeply meaningful conflicts and reconciliations.

18. Paul Tillich, *Systematic Theology*, Vol. 3 (Chicago: University of Chicago Press, 1963), p. 245. Cf. also his discussion of the "Gestalt of Grace" in Vol. 2 of *Systematic Theology*, pp. 163–207, and the discussion of "The Formative Power of Protestantism" in *The Protestant Era* (Chicago: University of Chicago Press, 1948), chapter 14.

19. Cf., e.g., Albert La Pierre, Bernard Verkamp et al., eds., *The Church: Readings in Theology* (New York: P. J. Kenedy and Sons, 1963), Hans Küng, *Structures of the Church* (New York: Thomas Nelson and Sons, 1964), and Karl Rahner, *Nature and Grace: Dilemmas in the Modern Church* (New York: Sheed and Ward, 1964).

The interest in clergy revealed by Powers and other writers is stimulated by the intention of bringing into fiction in a quick, direct way an indication of the spiritual illnesses and possibilities in American life. The illnesses are suggested in several ways. Most often they are suggested by the inability of a priest to assist the protagonist in his difficulty. The state of general spiritual dryness in the society is often expressed through the rendering of a priest who adds nothing helpful and often only exasperates a protagonist's spiritual quandary. The protagonist is thrown on his own resources when the chief proponent of spiritual wisdom and power is found to be a weak, troubled, or foolish man. The illnesses of the time may also be expressed in a clergyman who experiences grave misgivings, frustrations, and doubts because of his position or concerning his faith. If he is having trouble believing or maintaining hope, how much more should those have trouble who lack his spiritual training. The illness of the society can be rendered by the suggestion that the conflicts and personal antipathies which mark the society are found also among the clergy. When the spiritual life reconciles man to his brother as little as it reconciles him to himself or to God, how much more divided and antagonistic toward one another must be those lives which lack the fruits of spiritual discipline? Finally, the illnesses of the society can be suggested by the clergyman's inability to bring what he feels to be true or helpful to the society, when he finds that there is no audience able to hear or receive what he has to say or give. Powers has used the clergy in all of these ways, alerting us to similar motives for the presence of clergy in the works of other American writers.

Although some writers locate positive, creative possibilities in the life and work of the clergy, primarily the priests of fiction turn the protagonist toward personal and less institutional sources of spiritual strength. We shall see this happening in the work of Malamud, Updike, De Vries, and Styron. In the process of securing some private or nonconventional spiritual source, the clergy are important not only negatively, however, as grossly disappointing representatives of the spiritual resources they supposedly represent. They can provide the protagonist with models and a language which equip him to do priestly work on his own. A clear example of this is found in James Agee's *A Death in the Family*, where the characters have deeply meaningful spiritual experiences which are non-conventional but which are created by expectations and language which they receive from traditional priestly sources. Finally, and most generally, the priestly aspect of recent fiction which illuminates most often positive possibilities in the contemporary situation lies in the attitudes and work of those narrators who, by turning attention to some highly significant event, object, or set of experiences and by ordering a fictional world, duplicate or parallel the role of the priest in society. This close parallel may account more fully than one could document for the recurring interest in clergy revealed by the fiction writers of our time.

2

The Blood of the Lamb and the Sense of Transcendent Power

The question of transcendent power and its relation to human need and desire is one frequently raised by the narrators and characters of recent fiction. They feel coerced by forces which are more than or other than human, forces over which they have no control. Even when these forces are social or are exerted by the society, they are so ubiquitous and heavy-handed that the individual can do little to modify them or accommodate himself to them. These forces, whether ontological or social, an impersonal society or a hostile world, have created the experience of the absurd, the feeling that what a person most deeply desires and needs from or in his world is contradicted by what his world, social and natural, gives to him. Albert Camus has given most forceful expression to this feeling, but it is found in a good bit—one is tempted to say all—of our fiction. Resulting is the figure of the narrator or character intimidated or harassed by powers which lie beyond his control, the figure of the victimized or exiled antihero.

The works we are considering here are not exceptions to this general preoccupation in recent literature. Even in *Morte D'Urban*, where we find the least explicit involvement with transcendent power, the figures of Father Urban and Billy Cosgrove have a more than individual importance, since the two suggest, as do other characters, larger forces which are hostile to one another, forces of the society and Church of which these men are representatives and by which they are governed. And we shall see that John Updike's fiction, including *The Centaur*, discovers powers which puzzle and confuse his characters. Although such forces are more fully suggested in *The Poorhouse Fair, Rabbit Run,* and *Couples,* George and Peter Caldwell are threatened not only by other people and their uncertain positions, but also by influences they cannot control, especially death. A major concern of *The Fixer* is the potential in history and in society to confound the Jewish protagonist, a potential that is greater than any series of events or any group of people. And Styron's Nat Turner is a lonely man influenced by powers which lie beyond his control. The characters and narrators in these works struggle with, or are victims of, forces which are more or other than human. They live with a sense of transcendent power.

The Blood of the Lamb, while concerned with transcendent power, is, as we saw *Morte D'Urban* to be, often comic. De Vries is known as a comic writer, a writer placed in a position of having his manner or tone taken as more important than his material. This reputation may account for the fact that De Vries is a neglected American artist, the one writer addressed in this study who has not been given a major prize and who is not the subject of scores of critical essays. His reputation suggests that his work is of passing value because he uses material, presents problems and situations, in order to be funny about them. Occasionally he does; occasionally he seems to set up a situation in order to joke. But primarily De Vries's characters, situations, and problems are more important to his fiction and of more enduring value than his jokes, and his comedy, when it is most effective, arises out of his material. De Vries's interests in transcendent power and in characters distressed by it are not stimulated by his need for funny lines; he has, as we shall see, this constant concern in his fiction, and his humor does the work, first, of George Meredith's comic spirit, pricking the pride of those who feel that the powers have been tamed, and, second, the work of clarifying what the word "I" means in the face of coercion.

Transcendent power is not the only factor threatening self-identity in De Vries's fictional world. As in Updike and Malamud, the loss of a traditional religious orientation and the fact of high mobility result in characters torn from a surrounding, nurturing context. They are people, consequently, who do not derive content for self-identity from a culture with which they are deeply identified or which has very much of value to offer. So, while the problem created by transcendent power is very great, the answer that his protagonists and narrators must formulate is given little content by the cultural situation in which they live.

As we look at *The Blood of the Lamb* we should keep in mind that its mixture of serious problems with funny material is not unique to the De Vries corpus. This technique is shared by Barth, Pynchon, Heller, Vonnegut, and others. More importantly, we should try to clarify the cause of the problems and the role of the comic so that the effect of these two elements on one another and on the form of the work can be seen.

I

As in almost all of De Vries's work, tone, a subjective presence, is in control of *The Blood of the Lamb*, selecting material, anticipating later developments, and clarifying the significance of events. The work is a confessional fiction, and, as Northrop Frye has pointed out, confessional writing is prompted by a concern not so much for people and events as for some idea or problem. In *The Blood of the Lamb* the narrator provides continuity to the experiences of his life by referring them to a problem he has felt since his youth, the separation of human suffering from the answers to suffering proffered by science and religion.

If the parts of his life which the narrator shares with us do not concern moments of suffering or do not display the distance from suffering which religion and science maintain, they work toward developing a personal answer to suffering which is the narrator's own. What prompts the confession, then, is the problem of suffering's distance from scientific and theological answers and the highly personal answer to suffering which he and those he loved were at times able to achieve and share.

There is no difficulty in pointing out the problem in the book; suffering, religion, and medicine are constants. Don's intimates die —Louie, his father and mother, Rena Baker, his wife, and his daughter Carol. In addition, three hospitals are described with details of the people who languish and die there. Medical science is helpless in the face of this suffering. From Doc Berkenbosch, whose practice depends more on church membership than on medical skill, to Westminster Hospital, where the most advanced research is accused of doing little more than prolonging sickness, medical science is unable to touch human life at the moments of loss, pain, and death. Finally, religion is shown to aggravate the situation because it offers a God who should and could do something for man but refuses and who is, after all, in some way responsible for the whole affair. Religion and medical science preoccupy the narrator from beginning to end, offering their inadequate responses to human need, from Doc Berkenbosch and the Reverend Van Scoyen at the beginning to Westminster's research center and the Church of St. Catherine at the end.

More difficult to clarify are the moments in life which ameliorate suffering. But they are all-important to the narrator; in fact, such moments seem to create or condition the relationships with others to which as narrator he wants to bear a true and faithful witness. They are moments when his spirit is welded to another's, and they have to do with the juxtaposition of life and death or pain and joy.

The tone of the narration ranges between morbidity and unabashed spoofing, as between the details of Carol's disintegration and Don's remark to his girl friend that since he cannot decide which of her legs is the more beautiful the truth must lie somewhere in between. These extremes are intended to evoke a wide variety of responses in the reader. But joy and pain, the morbid and the funny, become significant when they are close together. Most often the resulting compound is a grotesque one, for the grotesque is, as he says, a "blend of the tragic and the comic":[1] leukemic children with party hats, his father's insanity, his wife's guilt feelings and religious conversions, Stein's satiric and cynical remarks. But occasionally, unexpectedly, the sad and joyful antitheses of life join to form moments of exquisite beauty and personal meaning, for people bound together in a common suffering find joy in a union

1. Peter De Vries, *The Blood of the Lamb* (Boston and Toronto: Little, Brown and Co., 1961), p. 115.

THE BLOOD OF THE LAMB

created by it. Such moments, Don's precious relationships with Louie, Rena, Greta, and Carol, are intimate because of death's proximity and are associated with beautiful things—flowers, snow, mountains, appreciative glances, and gentle touching.

The comic and the morbid do not only stand apart from one another, consequently, as some who have found fault with this book suggest. It is especially not true that the first part of the book is funny and the second part sad, creating a sharp break in the work and calling its unity into question. The pressure of loss is greater on the narrator at the end than at the beginning, but he loses throughout, and the answer which comic union within suffering provides is correspondingly more conclusive at the end than it is at the start.

Rather than two, there are three parts to the work, corresponding to three sections of Don's life. The sections are distinguishable because in them Don's attitudes toward himself and his world change.

The first part, from the opening through chapter six, is shaped by Don's interest in detaching himself from his origins. The biggest threat is getting enmeshed in the net of his religious and ethnic group, a group which Don increasingly sees as so culturally barbaric and so religiously authoritarian that its rigidity could imprison him forever in the confines of crudity. Marriage is the primary form of that threat, but Don also senses the community's less specific pressures for conformity and the frustrations of individual, free spirits who are repressed by them. Don concludes that his father is stuck in Chicago because he cannot face the possible seasickness of a voyage back to Holland and is faithful to the Church only because he needs the reduced fees at the hospital which membership allows. His brother Louie, another free spirit, has created, with his amorous and intellectual exploits, an inevitable separation from the community, while Doc Berkenbosch has cut the nerve of his protest because he needs the community's patronage.

Because the ethnic group from which he springs considers itself religiously to be identical with God's chosen people, Don's rejection of their life, his increasing insensitivity toward their judgment, and his quest for a more fashionable existence constitute for them an act of self-damnation. In this part he is between two worlds, a voyeur of both the community he rejects and the non-Dutch life he has not yet attained.

As a voyeur Don is able to maintain his critical distance on both worlds. He does not fall into the net of his own entrapping origins, but he also avoids the net of Hyde Park's strained sophistication. The Winklers are no improvement over the Wigbaldys. And as a voyeur he is able to see desirable aspects of each world, the aesthetic sensitivity, the beauty and grace in the worldly existence as well as the passionate interest in matters of the mind and spirit, the familial warmth, and the good fun with his brother and father which characterize his home.

Since he will allow neither world to absorb him, Don must develop the courage to create a personal alternative to both the religious and the nonreligious worlds. The strength to do that he receives from Louie. Although his parents felt that Don, the weaker brother, would be drained of his strength by Louie if they slept in the same bed, Louie imparted his strength to Don. Especially important is the freedom Louie gives Don from the fear of damnation which rejection of the community instills.

By Louie's dying, Don is enabled to see his family's religious response to calamity as an unsightly submission to a deified tyrant. The call to submit to this deity and to the form of his presence, the community of the elect, becomes for Don an odious, life-denying demand, and the only course available to him is to turn on both God and community in an act of heroic self-damnation. Don's act of rejecting his Dutch Reformed origins together with the world of Hyde Park's sophisticates implies a new stance of comic isolation maintained by his developing self-sufficiency.

In the second part of the book, from chapter six through chapter ten, Don learns that self-sufficiency is a vulnerable personal answer, and he is drawn into fellowship with like-suffering people of which his relationship with Louie was an incomplete precursor. Correspondingly, Don becomes increasingly aware in this part of transcendent powers at bay in the world which are able to disintegrate anything that is of value. At the denominational sanatorium in Colorado, Don realizes the vulnerability of his self-sufficiency. "It was then, for the first time," he tells us, "that the suspicion struck me that I might be sick."[2]

In the center of sickness and in a grotesque milieu of sexual (Hank Hoos) and religious (Cora Nyhoff) fanaticism, Don discovers a new form of personal association with Rena Baker, the sanatorium's fragile saint. Their relationship is a beautiful, stolen moment in an environment under the power of decay and death.

Once a voyeur himself, Don now resents those who look in at the beauty he experiences with Rena. He is now within, and his secretive relationship with Rena is the world of grace which all along he had sought. It is important that their most beautiful afternoon, in which their sexual experiences are ingredients in a larger, aesthetic whole, is an afternoon just before Rena's death. Don tells of that afternoon with her death in mind, and the delicate joy of their remembered last moment is heightened by the presence of darkness. This contrast between sadness or death and joy or beauty becomes increasingly important for his personal answer to human suffering.

The Thursday evening club at Dr. Simpson's home is also a beachhead of warm fellowship in a land of disease. Don's feeling for Dr. Simpson does not rise to the level of his experience with Rena until, having accused Dr. Simpson of being, in effect, a voyeur of death, he learns that the doctor lost a seven-year-old son to leukemia. Narrating later, Don realizes that at that time he lacked the maturity expressed by Simpson's distaste for Don's question on belief in God.

It took me some years to attain his mood and understand my blunder. He resented such questions as people do who have thought a great deal about them. The superficial and the slipshod have ready answers, but those looking this complex life straight in the eye acquire a wealth of perception so composed of delicately balanced contradictions that they dread, or resent, the call to couch any part of it in a bland generalization. The vanity (if not outrage) of trying to cage this dance of atoms in a single definition may give the weariness of age with the cry of youth for answers the appearance of boredom.[3]

2. Ibid., p. 81.
3. Ibid., p. 111.

It is the common suffering which creates in Don a new appreciation for the man.

Don next witnesses his father's disintegration and it is in contrast with this grotesque spectacle, "a blend of the tragic and the comic," that Don's warm memories of experiences with his father become meaningful. It is in the midst of this grotesqueness that Don takes up once more with Greta Wigbaldy.

The marriage with Greta is a necessary link for Don's narration between his involvement with his parents and his love for his daughter. As a necessary link it lacks individual significance. What is surprising is not so much the way he and Greta meet, renew their bond, marry and have their daughter; nor are Greta's guilt feelings, grotesque conversions, and suicide necessarily unconvincing; what is surprising and unconvincing is Don's attitude toward marriage, love, and death in this set of events. He is passive, distant, and cool about all these matters, and such attitudes are out of character for a man for whom getting married, making love, and sensing the presence of death were such deeply troubling and portentous matters. Perhaps the reason lies in Greta herself, but we are not prepared by anything in her to anticipate Don's unusual detachment. One may argue that the reason for this is that the episodes form a link between his youthful relationships, Louie, his father, and Rena and his adult, parental love. Or one may argue that Don's relationship with Greta is not fully or convincingly rendered because it is the least autobiographical of the materials which De Vries has given his narrator. But whatever the reason, although we would expect Greta to stand in the same light as Louie, Don's parents, Rena, and, later, Carol, she does not, and the relationship stands as too developed to be merely a link and too incomplete to stand with the rest.

The episodes presenting Greta's uneven emotional life also provide a bridge between the theological disputes of Don's home and his fencing over the question of God with Stein. In his arguments with the Reverend Tonkle, Greta's Fundamentalist pastor, Don leans heavily on Louie's words. This section is somewhat surprising and unconvincing, too, because Don seems to have advanced, by his experiences in Colorado, to a point where he would find an attack on the infirm basis of this man's convictions unnecessary. It is important to the work that Don should champion doubt at a point just before describing his relationship with Carol, but his attack on this barbaric revivalist makes him no champion.

In this set of episodes with Greta, Don seems to present the unfortunate consequences of the iconoclastic period of his life as they are seen in Greta. She has been affected by the breakdown of clear and rigid standards of sexual conduct and doctrinal beliefs, a breakdown to which Don contributed much. Although he is not responsible for her emotional problems or for her suicide, Don seems to suggest that his rejection of the simple but firm answers his background offered for conduct and belief was a risky move, since Greta could not make the same move with impunity. But Don's stance is so detached and his response to Tonkle so lacking in maturity that the presentation of this dark side, if the author intended it, does not come off. As though sensing this he hastens on to Carol, "Tuesday's Child, so full of grace, so poised that, as a friend of ours remarked, you could hold her on your outstretched palm and she would balance perfectly."[4]

In the third part, from the end of chapter ten to the close of the book, the father's exquisite sojourn with Carol is rendered. In that relationship the concerns of the whole work are brought into focus.

Before the nature of Carol's disease is fully known, Don establishes three things which become central to their relationship. The first is the child's beauty. She is a highly imaginative, unpredictable, sensitive child, and in stature she is perfect. Indeed, his relationship with her is everything to him; we are given little more of his adult life than this, and it is presented as a continual closeness which ordinary fathers achieve with their daughters only rarely.

The second matter is Don's answer to the question of the greatest experience available to man, an answer he has felt to be true at least since his love for Rena. Not physical but emotional experiences are of greatest importance, and the emotion Don selects is not the reward of achievement and not the feeling of being rescued from death but the experience of finding delight in one's world once

4. Ibid., p. 151.

more after conditions of threat and stress have been removed. A boy feels more joy in learning that his girl friend is not pregnant than he felt in the pleasure of his sexual relations with her. When one's normal world has been restored to him, a man appreciates afresh its hues and worth.

The third item secured at the beginning of this final part is Don's mature articulation of his philosophy of life, one he sends off to his college newspaper in answer to their request. This statement is so important to the narrator that he repeats it twice in full, once at this point and later by Carol's voice on the tape recorder. The philosophy is highly personal, and it articulates quite accurately what Don seems to have discovered by his experiences in Chicago and Colorado. With Dr. Simpson he recoils from any attempt to formulate what life means. Life is meaningful only when it is personal, and it becomes personal through beautiful human relationships. A person must create moments of beauty with other people, moments that can be created by cultivating the human trinity of "Reason, Courage, and Grace." Although Don departs from this statement by his outbursts of emotion and his quest for objective meaning during Carol's sickness, he returns to the statement at the end, and it stands as a plateau of conviction which he has achieved and beyond which he cares not to move. It is by his daughter's own manner during her suffering, her reason, courage, and grace during a time when, she tells him on the same recording, she knew what was happening, that Don realizes no greater grace could be given than the kind she had given him by the beautiful style of her personal life.

Don's two excursions beyond this plateau, the one quite rational, his debate with Stein, and the other irrational, his attacks on God, are supported by his former life and not by his relation to Carol. Of both responses to suffering, rational and irrational, Don is, by Carol's life and death, purged.

Stein's cynicism is consistent; he expects no more from science than he does from religion. His attitude is extreme, even grotesque, but Don is drawn to him because he acts in a manner that is far more honest than do those who adhere "to that sacred hoax to which we were now one and all committed down to the gates of death: the hoax that Everything Was Fine."[5] What Don does not share with Stein is not Stein's distaste for the way things are put together in this world; Don is very outspoken on what he considers to be the slaughter of innocents. Rather, he does not share Stein's confident, rational atheism; he wants to pull back from conclusions about hidden things, and Stein's convictions seem as ironclad as the theological assertions of Don's Dutch relatives.

Without Stein's grotesque humor, Don's depiction of leukemia's assault on Carol would be too much for the reader to bear. The victim is too helpless and the enemy is too well known to allow the reader to expect anything but the worst. And as I said before, the interest of the narrator is not only in the lives of those he loves; those lives are also placed in a larger context of concern for a response to the suffering of human life. Consequently, not as much attention is given to Carol's disintegration as to the way he and Carol could, in the face of death, squeeze "from each day what the frugal Mrs. Brodhag did from an orange—everything,"[6] or extort from simple things all their pleasures when once again their world together had been restored to them.

Don's second excursion beyond the plateau of his philosophical statement is assault on beauty and God. It is clearly an act outside his relation to Carol.

> The nobility, the reticence and dignity of that royal child cannot always be reported of the father. Dead-drunk and cold-sober, he wandered out to the garden in the cool of the evening, awaiting the coming of the Lord. No such advent taking place, he shook his fist at the sky and cried, "If you won't save her from pain, at least let me keep her from fear!" A brown thrush began his evening note, the ever favored, unendurable woodsong. I snatched up a rock from the ground and stoned it from the tree.[7]

The second irrational assault on God has more significance than such instances of rage. We are carefully prepared for it by Carol and Omar who have seen a sampling of old-style comedies at the

5. Ibid., p. 179.
6. Ibid., p. 185.
7. Ibid., pp. 203–4.

theatre. They specifically describe the pie-in-the-face routine. Carol asks Don whether he has noticed that

> ". . . after the one guy throws his pie and it's the other guy's turn, the first guy doesn't resist or make any effort to defend himself? *He just stands there and takes it.* He even *waits* for it, his face sort of ready?"[8]

Omar calls it a "ritual" and a "ceremony."

In his assault on God after Carol's death, when Don throws the cake at the statue of Christ, the statue seems to expect it, "his face sort of ready." Unlike the Promethean defiance of the first assault, this gesture makes God a participant in a ceremony of shared suffering. But these two assaults, the one naked and spontaneous, the other rich and imaginative, presuppose a fixed, transcendent object. However significant that presupposition may be and however rich in implication the assaults, especially the second, Don withdraws at the end from direct dealings with God. He returns to the holy ground of his dead loves.

Since it is the threat and presence of decay and death which allow the beauty and value of particular things to be revealed, the leave-takings which Don describes are epitomes of his celebration of moments which make life possible. It is to these poignant moments of taking leave that the narration continually moves and returns. I have already mentioned Louie's parting glance and Don's last afternoon with Rena. In the third part Don takes leave of his family and of Carol. They all, but especially the latter, form exquisite moments.

> The nurse stepped outside a moment, and I moved quickly from the foot of the bed around to the side, whispering rapidly in our moment alone:
>
> "The Lord bless thee, and keep thee: The Lord make his face shine upon thee, and be gracious unto thee: The Lord lift up his countenance upon thee, and give thee peace."
>
> Then I touched the stigmata one by one: the prints of the needles, the wound in the breast that had for so many months now scarcely ever closed. I caressed the perfectly shaped head. I bent to kiss the cheeks, the breasts that would now never be fulfilled, that no youth would ever touch. "Oh, my lamb."[9]

8. Ibid., p. 191.
9. Ibid., p. 234.

As has been said of J. D. Salinger's manner, De Vries walks at these critical moments a narrow path between silence and sentimentality.

The three parts of the work find their unity in the narrator himself; this is his book of the dead, and he is a "true and faithful witness." But the narration arises out of a desire both to preserve the memory of suffering loves and to give expression to the personal response to suffering which is offered by the human intimacy suffering creates, a response that makes life possible.

The chief alternative to this answer of human intimacy are the religious answers provided by Don's background, since those answers and their source are personal, too. But Don concludes that belief in God makes human suffering intolerable because God ought not to allow it. God, for Don, is objective transcendent power, and brute, destructive transcendent power must be defied. As he says:

> These displaced Dutch fisherfolk, these farmers peddling coal and ice in a strange land, must have had their reasons for worshiping a god scarcely distinguishable from the devil they feared.[10]

The God Don rejects is scarcely distinguishable from the devil because brute, transcendent power is intimidating and violent; the only decent thing to do is to defy it.

Don's view of God is aggravated by the fact that the question of God comes up most often when something unpleasant happens. Since God makes his appearance at times of suffering and death, Don's attitude toward God takes the form of a resentful "Why?" Since that question never gets answered, the way is made clear for Don to reject all speculations in this area, all attempts to establish a meaning for human suffering and life, and to embrace what is at hand, the potential for beauty in his own life and in his relationships with others.

Talk of God's relation to human suffering is also problematic because it contradicts the language of medical science. The doctors are not interested in ultimate questions, although Don brings such matters up to almost all of them. The language of the medical arts

10. Ibid., p. 25.

48

indicates causes which can be discerned and attacked. If God is a cause for suffering, he should be attacked too. But God cannot be attacked. Only two choices seem available, either to resist evil and forget about God or to accept God as causing human evil and providing its ultimate cure. Albert Camus's characters in *La Peste*, Rieux and Paneloux, present these two responses, and, as Camus himself has said, "only two possible worlds can exist for the human mind: the sacred (or, to speak in Christian terms, the world of grace) and the world of rebellion."[11]

Don's personal response to a world beset by cruel and unpredictable forces comes from his background, too, although it constitutes at the same time a way of rejecting what his relatives believed. Individual courage and the beauty of human intimacy marked his home. He calls his father a "fearless voyager" on the seas of doubt. And when Don's indifference toward tuberculosis is noticed by his neighbors, an indifference which we know is created by Don's desire to put some distance between himself and his girl friend, those around him considered it "a spectacle of grace and spirit which all who came under its spell found inspiring, a lesson worth taking to heart."[12] One has only to know how Calvin struggled with Stoic determinism to recall that Reformed theology with its predestinarian emphasis could easily produce people who were stoically prepared for the pains of immigrant experience. Don's parents, in their ability to suffer uncertain seas, to turn from their origins, and to make their way toward a land they had never seen, create an emigrant capacity in the son whose fictional voyage is difficult and long. And the pleasure "extorted from Simple Things when the world has once again been restored to you"[13] is Don's version of the joy his father felt when "he fell on his knees and kissed the American soil for no other reason than that it was not open water."[14]

The beauty and value of human intimacy is also a gift to Don

11. Albert Camus, *The Rebel* (New York: Alfred A. Knopf, 1954), pp. 26–27.
12. De Vries, *The Blood of the Lamb*, p. 78.
13. Ibid., p. 166.
14. Ibid., p. 3.

49

from his parents. The religious and ethnic agreement created a level of communication which makes the relationships Don sees in the non-Dutch world look superficial and unsatisfying. And the moments when he experiences personal joy and fellowship with another human being are precious to him because they remind him of home. In developing his personal answer to suffering, Don accepts and rejects aspects of both the religious and the nonreligious worlds. He turns from the rationalism and hypocrisy of both, and he derives content for his personal answer from whatever honesty and capacity for feeling he has found in either one.

II

What is most characteristic of recent fiction may not be, as many have insisted, the loss of the hero and the rise of the nonhero; rather, it may be the loss of a personal antagonist. What the principal characters of recent fiction are up against is not so much an identifiable or personal enemy or opponent as an impersonal, pervasive, and oppressive power. With the loss of an antagonist we find the loss of the protagonist or hero. Without an identifiable, personal opponent, the strengths and individuality of the protagonist cannot be actualized. Pitted against forces which are beyond his control, which are, even, impossible to name, the protagonist is intimidated or victimized, and whatever life he can secure for himself must be secured in spite of and not in communication with whatever it is that opposes him. A clear instance of this shift in recent fiction from a personal to an impersonal enemy can be seen in that very influential book, Albert Camus's *La Peste*. Camus chose not to write about the Germans but to translate his war experience into a fiction in which the opponent is experienced as an impersonal, constant, dehumanizing power. The sense of transcendent power, of a power over which the principal character has no control and which poses a threat either to his very existence or to its meaning, is common to recent fiction.

Often this threatening, impersonal power is more social than natural or metaphysical. In terms of Camus's characters, the vision of the plague is more like Tarrou's than like Doctor Rieux's. Although the intimidating power resides in or is expressed by the social structure, it is not for that reason less impersonal, for the aggregate will is something more than a sum of personal wills, and the individual cannot even locate, much less influence, that aspect of the society which threatens to undo him.

De Vries in all of his fiction joins the others in this study, especially Malamud, and many more in this country, Heller, Barth, Vonnegut, and Hawkes to name a few, whose characters feel that they have been thrust into a world which is either disappointing or is antagonistic to their own or to all human life. If there are redeeming features or experiences in life, such as laughter or close communication, they are isolated and hard won.

It may seem strange to put a discussion of De Vries's fiction in the context of so-called absurdist literature or literature of despair. De Vries is so often taken lightly. At times he seems to deserve this treatment, since at times he appears to subject his fiction to his humor rather than to subject his humor to his art. But primarily his humor does serve his fiction, and his interest in revealing the whole truth about American experience and the absurdities of human life is serious business indeed. The comedy has primarily two important roles, to prick illusion or to laugh down what is grotesque in American life and to provide his protagonists with a stouthearted stand against a cruelly intimidating and disappointing world.

In his earlier works, De Vries's protagonists are relatively self-confident. They have this confidence because they stand in opposition to evils they can identify and from which they can be free. Primarily the evils are associated with the conventional, provincial, or unenlightened mind of the group. In contrast to the herd, these characters strive for the precious prize of an Oscar Wilde style. Disdaining the public mind, bearing *Weltschmerz* and speaking in puns and paradoxes, these aesthetes avoid the strictures of marriage and a steady job. Augie Poole in *The Tunnel of Love* (1954), Chick Swallow in *Comfort Me With Apples* (1956), The Reverend Mackerel in *The Mackerel Plaza* (1958), and Sweetie Appleyard in *The Tents of Wickedness* (1959)[15] secure their confident individuality by rejecting the herd and by looking toward an ideal suggested by such names as "Wise Acres" and "Moot Point," a world of "Babylonian grace" that, while never achieved, is ever the goal. However, the comic element in these works does not reside only in these aesthetes' disdain for the mass; the comedy arises, in the manner of George Meredith, in the obviously egotistic stance of these characters, and the pleasure given the reader is derived both from laughing at those things the aesthete disdains and then laughing at him, since he has achieved an egotism which cannot go unchecked.

The characters in these works are also sensitive to human need, and their ministry to misery adds grace to their witty *savoir faire*. Chick Swallow is a kind of Miss Lonelyhearts, and even People's Liberal Church, despite its quaint modernity, is geared to meet human needs. This sensitivity to human need saves the characters from the charge of irresponsibility which Chick Swallow brings against Sweetie Appleyard.

A third recurring interest of these characters is in morality. Several stories in *No, But I Saw the Movie*[16] (1952) move around people's feelings of guilt and morality, and a dominant theme of *The Tunnel of Love* is that our vices often have the reverse effect of making us moral. This interest in morality is most clearly expressed by the role marriage plays in these works. Beginning with his first book, *But Who Wakes the Bugler?*[17] (1940), and in all his early work, De Vries's characters move within, from, or towards marriage. Marriage is an expression of a morally ordered world, and when marriage fails, as it does in *Through the Fields of Clover*[18] (1961), the confidence and laughter of his characters are

15. Peter De Vries, *The Tunnel of Love* (Boston: Little, Brown and Co., 1954), *Comfort Me With Apples* (Boston: Little, Brown and Co., 1956), *The Mackerel Plaza* (Boston: Little, Brown and Co., 1958), and *The Tents of Wickedness* (Boston: Little, Brown and Co., 1959).

16. Peter De Vries, *No, But I Saw the Movie* (Boston: Little, Brown and Co., 1952).

17. Peter De Vries, *But Who Wakes the Bugler?* (Boston: Houghton Mifflin Co., 1940).

18. Peter De Vries, *Through the Fields of Clover* (Boston: Houghton Mifflin Co., 1961).

lost. Marriage and morality fail in this book because faith in a transcendent meaning or order has broken down.

This breakdown marks a transition in the De Vries corpus. In the earlier work confidence in a meaning higher than human design supports morality and humor. *The Tunnel of Love* ends in resignation to a design by which the characters are governed. The summation at the close of *Comfort Me With Apples* is a recitation of a restored universal order. And the Reverend Mackerel comments at the end, "You can't say there isn't such a thing as a designing intelligence."[19] Characters in the later novels lack this confidence. Beginning with *Through the Fields of Clover* they must maintain their morality and comic stance only on the basis of their personal sympathy and strength.

In *Reuben, Reuben*[20] (1964), the principal characters of all three parts are entirely on their own and not doing very well. Spofford falls victim to the creeping menace of suburbia; McGland concludes that God is to be blasphemed for his insensitivity to human suffering; and Mopworth falls victim to chaos as the structures of marriage and morality crumble. With the loss of confidence in an ordering, transcendent design, the characters of De Vries's later fiction can guard their humor, compassion, and morality in nothing more than themselves, and, as we have seen, this attempt becomes a central concern in *The Blood of the Lamb*.

In his more recent work, the sense of transcendence has more the character of that found in Don Wanderhope's experience or in McGland's. Rather than supporting a world that conforms to a man's intentions and desires, the transcendent power his characters experience is insensitive to, or even hostile toward, their best interests. Almost taking this situation for granted, his later characters become stouthearted opponents or comic victims of the situation. Tom Waltz in *Let Me Count the Ways*[21] (1965), for example, is a comical combination of his Fundamentalist mother and atheist father, and he has no place to go. A grotesquely pious agnostic, he is lost in and at odds with his world. Irreverently pious and faith-

19. De Vries, *The Mackerel Plaza*, p. 260.
20. Peter De Vries, *Reuben, Reuben* (Boston: Little, Brown and Co., 1964).
21. Peter De Vries, *Let Me Count the Ways* (Boston: Little, Brown and Co., 1965).

fully blasphemous, he gets sick as a pilgrim in Lourdes. Joe Sandwich in *The Vale of Laughter*[22] (1967) is a victim of similar parentage and makes do by turning everything into a joke. The only trace of interest in a universal design is Joe's faint nostalgia, and the narrator abandons his quest for transcendent reassurance, feeling "swept remorselessly out to sea while we spread our arms to the beautiful shore."[23] Without transcendent meaning, existence is baffling. Even though Joe becomes in the second part the butt as well as the perpetrator of jokes, his upending is not a reversal of his decision on universal meaning. Similarly, Professor Henry Tattersall in *The Cat's Pajamas*[24] (1968) is from the beginning in a very unsteady position. He fears disorder, feels overevaluated by his wife, dreads being laughed at, and is constantly criticized by his second self. Although he tries to stabilize himself by adopting the identities dictated by a number of jobs he takes, the professor slowly disintegrates until he can finally find peace only by ascetically renouncing all things and acting as absurdly as his world, selling cans of fresh air, giving literary lectures to an idiot boy, and composing tongue twisters. He comes to his end in death by cold and exposure, stuck in an entrance he had made for the dog. Henry calls attention to the absurdity of his world; in the midst of chaos he tries to do nice, little things for people. With this program he achieves personal peace and dies laughing. The second part of the book, *Witches' Milk*, is very similar to *The Blood of the Lamb* in its rendering of gratuitous suffering and resulting despair. With the loss of her son, Tillie Seltzer becomes isolated from and vicious toward her world. Despite her prayer, Tillie finds peace not in some transcendent power but by taking back her estranged husband. In the fiction he wrote in the sixties, then, De Vries's characters become less and less confident in the supportive potential of transcendent power. In fact, they find their lives threatened by powers which are indefinite and hostile, and it is in spite of these powers that the redeeming moments of laughter and human inti-

22. Peter De Vries, *The Vale of Laughter* (Boston: Little, Brown and Co., 1967).
23. Ibid., p. 216.
24. Peter De Vries, *The Cat's Pajamas and Witches' Milk* (Boston: Little, Brown and Co., 1968).

macy must be achieved. Lest we take all of this too seriously, however, De Vries gives us, with *Mrs. Wallop* (1970), an elbow in the ribs, a deflating attack by his middle-aged, mid-American mother figure on all, especially Existentialists and myth chasers, who impute to themselves a scope and glory they do not intrinsically possess.[25]

In tracing the changing nature of transcendent power in De Vries's fiction, I have neglected the better part of his work, the jokes, the crazy situations, the parodies of Shakespeare, Dylan Thomas et al., the puns, twists, and falls, and the engaging, playful tone of many of his narrators. De Vries is fun, and the humor is the most obvious element of his work. I have neglected this more obvious element to get at other sides of his characters, their individuality, sensitivity to human need, and moral self-consciousness. I have tried to point out that the atmosphere of his work changed so that these personal qualities in the second half of his corpus are grounded not on some transcendent power which supports human life but are established against transcendent powers which are impersonal and disruptive.

III

De Vries and some of his characters derive their interest in transcendent power from their Dutch Calvinist background. Formative for that background are the theological emphases of John Calvin and the Canons of Dort. But we ought to see that the heavy emphasis on transcendent power characteristic of this tradition is not limited to it, and the doctrines of predestination or of election are theological expressions of religious attitudes that cross the boundaries of separate traditions.

For Calvin, decision-making was a central attribute of God, and his use of a political metaphor, sovereignty, suggests the determining activity of the divine will. For Calvin, the primary obligation of the Christian mind was to give justice to the priority of divine decision-making.

25. Peter De Vries, *Mrs. Wallop* (Boston: Little, Brown and Co., 1970), p. 308.

Calvin was too much of a humanist to be unaware of forms of deterministic thought, especially Stoicism. He distinguished God's decision-making from determinism by elevating all causes to the realm of mystery.[26] Further, since God's decisions are to be apprehended first of all in Christ and through faith,[27] they can be or are for the believer always meaningful and beneficial.

A more extreme attitude toward transcendent power is revealed by the Canons of the Synod of Dort (1618–19), a document forming one of the creedal standards in the church of De Vries's youth. It is from these Canons more than from Calvin that ideas such as unconditioned election and total human depravity, ideas close to the heart of Don Wanderhope's parents, are derived. While such ideas make the Synod of Dort look like the nadir of Calvinistic anti-humanism, we should remember that these conclusions were drawn up not by some morbid recluse but by a distinguished ecumenical Reformed Council which met in an enlightened nation during that nation's most progressive century.[28]

The Synod of Dort was called in response to the work of Jacobus Arminius, a theologian who had taken in the name of faith a steadfast stand against the doctrine of predestination, and out of that stand, after his death, an Arminian creed, the Remonstrance, was drawn up (1610). The articles of this creed introduce what are essentially Pelagian ingredients into the understanding of man's relation to God. Arminius and his followers felt that the doctrine of predestination robbed Christian life of human initiative and freedom of will.

In uncompromising fashion the Synod of Dort responded by excluding from its formulation of man's relation to God any consideration of human activity. It reasserted predestination, limited Christ's atoning work to the Elect, emphasized the thoroughgoing

---

26. Cf. John Calvin, *Concerning the Eternal Predestination of God*, trans. J. K. S. Reid (London: James Clark and Co., 1961), especially pp. 170–78.

27. Cf. Edward Dowey, Jr., *The Knowledge of God in Calvin's Theology* (New York: Columbia University Press, 1952), especially p. 188.

28. "It was undoubtedly an imposing assembly; and, for learning and piety as respectable as any ever held since the days of the Apostles" (Philip Schaff, *The Creeds of Christendom* [New York: Harper and Brothers, 1881], p. 514).

corruption of man, and made God wholly responsible for the maintenance within grace of those he had saved.

The doctrines of predestination and total depravity have their proper context in a discussion of human sin and God's forgiveness. The delegates to the Synod felt that embedded in the Arminian position were elements calculated to dilute the gracious, gratuitous character of divine forgiveness. Apparently, it struck them as impossible to discuss God's gracious will and at the same time to talk about man in anything but a negative way. Since predestination and total depravity are doctrines which make sense only in a discussion of God's forgiveness, they become, when taken out of that context, highly problematic; as general propositions about human nature they will not do because they deny what is obvious from experience, the potential and initiative of human life. Further, these doctrines cannot be used in order to elevate one group of people above another, those who know they are totally depraved and elected standing above those happy but depraved humanists of the world who are joyfully marching to doom.[29] Don's relatives distort the doctrines in both ways. They use them as general, descriptive statements, and they use them to maintain the separate, privileged character of their own ethnic and religious group.

Don's relatives are consistent with their theological manner when they reject the theory of evolution, for the Calvinist-Arminian controversy is very similar to the Creation-evolution debate. The two problems are no longer debated not because they are solved but only because people in an ecumenical and tolerant era avoid arousing old disputes. The problem remains, and it is similar in both discussions. The Calvinists, like "Creationists," emphasize the activity, the will and power, of God and correspondingly de-emphasize the activity, development, and freedom of natural and human life. Pelagians, Arminians, and evolutionists recognize the self-creating potential in human and natural life, and to make room for this potential they must understand God as somewhat passive to, or withdrawn from, human actions.

29. For a brilliant analysis of the Arminian controversy and of the negative use of the doctrine of election, cf. Karl Barth, *Church Dogmatics*, Vol. II/2, "The Doctrine of God," trans. G. W. Bromiley et al. (Edinburgh: T. and T. Clark, 1957), pp. 34–76.

It is important to see, then, that the ideas of predestination and election are not idiosyncratic of one rather small tradition in Protestantism. The ideas, or attitudes behind them, are general. Historians of religion and anthropologists, for example, have clarified how significant the category of divine will is for primitive and ancient people. The gods for ancient man are personifications of power, and when order and peace exist in the world these states are special divine creations.

> To the Mesopotamian . . . cosmic *order* did not appear as something given; rather it became something achieved—achieved through a continuous integration of the many individual cosmic wills, each so powerful, so frightening. His understanding of the cosmos tended therefore to express itself in terms of integration of wills, that is, in terms of social orders such as the family, the community, and, most particularly, the state. To put it succinctly, he saw the cosmic order as an order of will—as a state.[30]

The creation of order and peace, delivery from destruction and chaos, is, then, always a wonder, the consequence of wills and decisions to which the religious man is not privy.

Rudolf Otto, in his discussion of the holy as an essential part of religious experience, calls the idea of election "an immediate and pure expression of the actual religious experience of grace."[31] Far from being a Calvinistic idea, Otto finds it expressive of religious experience itself. This is also true of the idea of predestination, "for the religious conception in the notion of predestination is nothing but that 'creature-consciousness,' that self-abasement and the annulment of personal strength and claims and achievements in the presence of the transcendent, as such."[32] The religious man is, according to Otto, always aware of a transcendent will which is prior to and superior to his own, and his own life and will become possibilities because of the divine will's gratuitous decision.

30. Thorkild Jacobsen, "The Cosmos as a State" in *Before Philosophy: The Intellectual Adventure of Ancient Man* (Baltimore: Penguin Books, 1949), pp. 139–40.
31. Rudolf Otto, *The Idea of the Holy,* trans. John W. Harvey (New York: Oxford University Press Galaxy Edition, 1958), p. 87.
32. Ibid., pp. 88–89.

THE SENSE OF TRANSCENDENT POWER

While the characters of De Vries's works have a sensitivity for transcendent power, they have an orientation towards it which is quite different from that of Calvin and other religious or theological attitudes and formulations. They do not feel, as did Calvin and others, that the presence of divine power is found first of all in some particular form.

A religious people is primarily impressed by the presence of God in a particular form. In that form they sense his power, and because of their proximity to that form their own place and time are ordered. Consequently, the people are first of all concerned with that particular form, thankful for its presence, aware of its awesome power, and surprised that it should be there at all and that it should enhance the people's life rather than condemn, reject, or destroy it. Subsequently, they begin to enlarge on themes derived from that particular form; the God who meets people in a particular way not only delivers them from the enslavement of darkness and evil but also gives them all things.

The characters in *The Blood of the Lamb* and in De Vries's other works do not think in this way. For one thing, they move from the general to the particular. Belief in Creation rather than in evolution and belief that God controls sickness and health are prior to belief that God brings people into his own life through and in a particular form. Their theology is derived not as much from the authoritative form as from their need for information about their world and their sicknesses, and the conclusion they draw is that God caused these things. This is clear when such ideas are presented as facts about the world rather than as ways of praising or celebrating God's power. As facts about the world they must be defended against other, conflicting facts. In their arguments Don's relatives are not speaking religiously; they use religious language to do scientific work. In addition, the things they say which are so authoritative for them, that God created the world or that man is a sinner, are cold, hard statements of a philosophical, historical, and anthropological nature. They are propositions about the way things are; they are not cries of men who have come to realize what God is.

Religious people not only move from the particular to the general when they talk about God, they also talk about the particular in terms of its life-enhancing intention. What gives rise to worship is the surprise that the divine, which is so awesome, should be here with us and we are not consumed. This is not because the divine has cooled off or has gotten old. The divine could and, perhaps, should destroy man, but the divine decides instead to tolerate him and, even, to let man share in the power and order which flow out from its presence. Certainly the presence of the divine has a dark side, and there is no possibility of presuming that a man can with impunity disregard that dark side. As soon as a man begins to count on or manipulate that presence, the divine may withdraw or destroy him. But the presence is not primarily to destroy; it is not an invasion. The forms of God's presence are creations, and a people's life is re-created and made meaningful and peaceful when it conforms to that presence. The Bible is quite consistent on this point. God is present for the purpose of forgiveness and life, although he is always present on his own terms.

When a religious people considers the particular form of divine presence as a gift, they understand the good to be gratuitous and evil to be constant. That man is born to suffer or that he lives in an evil world is a kind of first premise for religious life. Evil is the given. In this sense, evil is for the religious man more stable and predictable than good. What is evil, chaotic, unknown, intimidating, and meaningless is what the divinely created form dispels; the divine form is an act of deliverance from evil.

De Vries's characters tend to see both evil and good events as gratuitous. But the one sort, evil ones, they tend to associate with God, and the other sort, good ones, they attribute to human grace, courage, and beauty. Evil events are the primary gratuitous experiences of their lives. Life, for Don, for example, is basically good, and when something unfortunate happens this event must be attributed to some agency, a divine one. Don gets very angry with God, then, when his life is disrupted. God, in the world of these characters, is not associated with life and peace but with disruption and death.

THE SENSE OF TRANSCENDENT POWER

In the later fictions, De Vries's characters see evil occurrences as not such singular, isolated events. They suffer so many losses that they give up God's world of deprivation and death and opt for the human world of joy and intimacy, a world which stands opposed to the world of change or decay. God is associated with evil; mirth and human beauty, holy moments which redeem life from sadness, are human creations.

De Vries's later fiction, presenting as it does human life as an achievement against a background of violent forces over which man has no control, is consistent with a growing body of American literature in the sixties, although it can probably be said that ours has not been a literature marked with the kind of despair, sense of hostile transcendent powers, and the experience of the absurd that has characterized the dominant vision of European literature. We have not had our Kafkas and Sartres and Camuses and Becketts. But the attitude summarized by the word "absurd" has increasingly come to mark our literature, and *Catch-22*, *The Floating Opera*, *Second Skin*, and *One Flew Over the Cuckoo's Nest* have become representative of a growing trend. But even in the bleaker portion of recent American fiction, the vision of absurdity has often been balanced by human intimacy or humor; catastrophe is more often personal and social than ontological; and some of our most influential writers, while attentive to absurdity, have been more affirmative than bleak: James Agee, J. D. Salinger, Saul Bellow, and the other writers treated in this study.

Against this background, the contributions of Peter De Vries can be measured. He has moved with the period from a mood of confidence, through great uncertainty, and to a sense of hostile transcendent power, and he has made these moves on his own. With his mixture of the comic and the pathetic and its result, the grotesque, he stands with that group of writers commonly, and perhaps mistakenly, called black humorists. But what is impressive about him is that he derives his bleak vision from his own background and experiences, and his humor, while more disciplined and concentrated in the sixties than in the fifties, has been a mark of his writing since he began.

The world of De Vries's major characters is problematic basically because it is torn. The separated components can be suggested geographically by Chicago and Connecticut. Chicago represents immigrant isolation, the parochial, peasant mentality surrounding the youth of De Vries himself and many of his characters. Connecticut represents the slick, nonreligious, enlightened mentality which attracts and intimidates the boy in Chicago and finally draws him out of his father's faith and home.

What De Vries has not been able to do in his fiction is to suggest that the Chicago origins, with their incestuous cultural and religious inversion, are all bad and that Eastern exurbia, with its forms of rebellion and relativity, is all good. Certainly, Chicago had its faults, its pride and life-denying authoritarianism. But unlike the decent denizens of Connecticut, those folk never lacked deeply personal interrelationships. Perhaps they suffered from overidentity by making their existence synonymous with truth and the work of God in the world. But De Vries sees the uncertainty of moderns as no less pathetic than the Fundamentalist mentality he deplores. The desperate search for intimacy in Decency, Connecticut, where communication, not to speak of love, is hardly possible because neighbors lack shared values and meaning, is no improvement. The old-fashioned and the avidly contemporary alternatives of American life are both deficient, and their juxtaposition creates for his characters a torn or troubled world.

The important point is not that these two worlds are exposed in their faults, although they are ruthlessly satirized. The point is that by not rejecting one for the other De Vries implies that there is something in each that holds him. What seems to be of value to so many of his characters and which was found in that Chicago home is belief. And what seems to be so forceful about the moderns is not their psychological theories or their metaphysic of fun but their tolerance and honesty. Religious convictions and contemporary uncertainty cannot be easily joined.

A middle course, what Tom Waltz in *Let Me Count the Ways* calls "Laodiceanism," being "lukewarm and neither hot nor cold,"[33]

33. De Vries, *Let Me Count the Ways,* p. 123.

is distasteful to De Vries, it seems, as is also the Mackerel manner, a thin or insipid religious humanism. In many of his novels the two forms of faith are separated, at times by caricature, e.g., the vulgar evangelicalism of street-corner preachers and the shallow humanism of Mackerel and his kind. The language of grace posted in phosphorescent letters or pasted by Tom Waltz to his enemies' car bumpers stands in sharp contrast to the language of the clever high priests of contemporary glamour and religious superficiality. In caricaturing the two, De Vries has illuminated their incompatibility.

The orientation of the old-fashioned religion is to the language of sin and grace, and it contradicts its modern, humanist alternative. The certainty of a community governed by the dialectic (if not the experience) of sin and grace and the relativity of a community governed by the fashions of contemporary culture form two divergent kinds of life. In *The Blood of the Lamb*, the problem is put in an extreme form because it discovers a man driven against the problem by the loss of those he loves. Rather than use either the God-language of his background or the language of human problem-solving, Don turns from the alternatives and from the problem of their relationship to the firmer ground of his memories and love.

3.

The Centaur and the
Problem of Vocation

Work is a burden for many characters in recent fiction not because
it is hard to do but because of the questionable nature of the work
itself; the work a character is asked to do so often has no direct
relation to his personal interests. Because their jobs and their personal interests do not support and enrich one another, characters
find themselves doing work which has no meaning or fleeing the
work they have been given to do.

Characters in John Updike's fiction find their jobs to be terribly
tiring and enervating, and work, whether it is teaching or selling or
carpentry, provides no positive resource for the characters in their
efforts to establish themselves before some threat or to formulate an
answer to some problem. Even the pastors in his novels and short
stories do not seem confident about what their jobs ask them to do
or be. From the inmates of *The Poorhouse Fair*, who have no place
of their own and no work, through Rabbit Angstrom and Joey
Robinson, to Piet Hanema in *Couples*, we find characters who must
do work they dislike and work that humiliates them, or who can no
longer do the kind of work they once did and enjoyed, or who run
away from their work.

The problem of work may at first appear to be a rather narrow
interest with which to address *The Centaur* and Updike's other fiction, but we should remember that work suggests more than a person's job; it suggests the whole range of responsibilities which a
person feels are pressed upon him, including his relation to his

family and friends. Work suggests his position in life, all of his offices. In addition to being inclusive, the topic of work has great depth, since it raises the question of personal integrity, of unity between what a person is and what he does; when conflict arises between what a person is or wants to be and what he does or is required to do, the conflict is a significant one. It is that conflict which lies at the center of most of Updike's fiction and at the center as the problem in one of his confessional fictions, *The Centaur*.

I

As *Morte D'Urban* has some of the characteristics of that form of fiction Northrop Frye and others call the "novel," so *The Centaur*, although it is finally confessional in form, is to a great degree also a romance. A variegated piece of work, it is Hawthornian in form, a work in which the fanciful and the real are held in tension and, at points, merged. We find fanciful descriptions of human actions and relationships in terms of Greek mythology suspended above, and, at times, touching and enlarging realistic descriptions of George Caldwell, teacher, husband, and father, and his artistic son, Peter. The fictional world Updike has built, then, has a split in it like a centaur's body, one part of it "afloat in a starry firmament of ideals" and the other "sunk in a swamp."[1] The two parts join when the mythological descends to be incarnate in the real or when the real opens itself to receive the myth. The structure that houses this contrast between and mixing of myth and reality is its confessional form.

The tone, the subjective presence, is provided by Peter. The story is finally his responsibility, although not all of it is narrated by him in the first person, because he is involved in what he tells through his nostalgia for a life that was good, that was "lived in God's sight," and because he is brought to a comparison between what he remembers and what he now is. As an adult in his canvas-cluttered New York loft, he asks, *"Was it for this that my father gave up his life?"*[2]

1. John Updike, *The Centaur* (New York: Alfred A. Knopf, 1963), p. 4.
2. Ibid., p. 270.

While anchoring this strange world with its real and fanciful elements, Peter's narration also participates in that strangeness. He is at the same time both disturbingly real and mythologically fanciful. When he thinks of himself as Prometheus, Chiron's charge, he is not simply the son of an average high school teacher. When the sores of his psoriasis appear to him "as if pecked by a great bird," he is not simply an anxious boy with an embarrassing malady. When he wears his red shirt, "a giant spark," and when he thinks of himself as chained to a rock and exposed, he is not simply another self-conscious adolescent. He is Prometheus-Peter.

A third structural element, in addition to the qualities of the romance and the narrator's confession, is the work's abstract expressionism, the presentation of emotion and ideas along the clearly outlined qualities of time and space. Within a geometric framework, private emotions are elevated. As in the works of Vermeer which Peter adores, what is personal, ordinary, or momentary is housed within geometrically described eternities, space and time.

Peter, for example, is very conscious of his temporal relation to what he is telling and of the power of time. All this takes place in January of 1947 on a Thursday, Monday, Tuesday, and Wednesday. It is now fifteen years later. Time controls the story because it separates Peter from the object of his narration and unifies the object; his experience with his father stands with all its richness within the boundaries of those few days.

As much as time, space is a significant factor in the work. To young Peter, for example, New York City is the future. In her museums New York holds the sacramental presence of art pieces Peter has seen only in reproduction. But at the moment of his narrating, the space values are reversed, and, surrounded by his canvases in New York, Peter looks back at Olinger and extends his personal emotion and question in the Vermeer of his narration. The Real Presence now becomes his father whom before Peter had never touched, but who now, as those museum masterpieces before, becomes a "profound mystery" within touching distance. His father now is given the aesthetic power Peter in his youth had attributed to New York's art.

THE PROBLEM OF VOCATION

George Caldwell is a man who has trouble accepting his offices as teacher, husband, father, and son. He does not hold his job as a general science teacher with any confidence. Painfully aware of his inadequacies, of student feelings, and the principal's power, he fears his dismissal. He is no more confident as a husband and father. He is afraid of sex; he resents his wife's decision to live in the country; he has trouble understanding his son. And George is deeply resentful toward his own father who died without religious confidence and left his family in debt.

Yet, in spite of all his troubled feelings, George is a strong and self-assertive man. He walks with "pressured, stoic grace." He bears pain without complaint and, refusing to lean on the strong shoulder of Al Hummel while the mechanic removes the arrow from George's leg, he stands stoically erect. He makes his way to school, the "hate factory," vigorously, prepared for the worst, and he faces his classes with resolute determination.

Finally, George is a deeply charitable man. Religiously he believes that "God made Man as the last best thing in His Creation."[3] With that kind of respect for people, he volunteers assistance, we are told, out of a "usual impulsive Christianity," and to conversations he brings "a cavernous capacity for caring that dismayed strangers."[4] Twice he even transcends conventional morality to express his charitable interest in people. To Peter's chagrin, for example, George chooses to ignore the fact that the hitchhiker they pick up is a homosexual, and George engages him in conversation. The same thing happens when he and Peter are met by a drunkard. This suspecting man accuses George of leading Peter to perversions, but despite the man's ugly suspicions of him, George chooses conversation with him above personal defense. George's charitable attitude toward people, his humility, distresses his son.

Peter has qualities that correspond to his father's. He is, for example, insecure; he is threatened by homosexuality; he dreads his father's possible death; he is so given to daydreaming and is so

3. Ibid., p. 63.
4. Ibid., pp. 82–83.

enamored with the future that the present seems meager in comparison. Both Peter and his father dislike physical things; Peter prefers Vermeer to 4–H, and, like George, Peter is dependent on his father.

Peter is also self-assertive and confident. Like his father, he is always "performing for an unseen audience."[5] Although as the son of a teacher he is mocked by other students, Peter thinks this mockery provides him elevation above the faceless mass of younger students. Even his psoriasis puts him in a select group with his mother and Dr. Appleton.

Peter has no moral confidence, however, and here too he is dependent on George. He is very disturbed by his father's conversations with the hitchhiker and the drunkard. And the narrating Peter seems not to have gained his father's religious humility and strength. In juxtaposition to a past "lived in God's sight," Peter's adult present leaves in his stomach "a sour wash of atheism."[6]

The story of father and son, together with the elements in the work of romance, the confessional form, and its abstract expressionism, are so radically involved in the work's architectonics that any meaning the work may have will lie in these formative elements.

Corresponding in the work to what I have called its abstract expressionism, the geometric lines of time and space, is the problem which is crucial to the story. Put simply, it is this: What can a person do to face the intimidating power of time and space?

In an exchange with his father-in-law, George puts the matter nicely. Pop Kramer likes proverbs, and one of them that is particularly irksome to George is the familiar "time and tide . . . wait for no man." "Did you ever stop to think," George says, "does any man wait for time and tide?"[7] The platitude implies that man is a victim of natural forces, and George finds that hard to take. As he says, "I was a minister's son. I was brought up to believe, and I still believe it, that God made Man as the last best thing in his

5. Ibid., p. 64.
6. Ibid., p. 46.
7. Ibid., p. 62.

Creation. If that's the case, who are this time and tide that are so almighty superior to us?"[8]

Although George sounds secure in the Christian doctrine that man is more important than natural forces, it soon becomes clear that things are not so simple for him. For one thing, the faith of his father from which that understanding comes is itself a cause for concern. His father died without faith's confidence, and George is afraid he too will lose his faith. In addition, George's scientific ideas stand at a distance from Christian doctrine. While describing the origins of human life, George displays to his students the opinion that in the natural process man holds an extremely tenuous and problematic position relative to time and space: "One minute ago, flint-chipping, fire-kindling, death-foreseeing, a tragic animal appeared . . . called Man."[9] Here man is not the culminating consequence of a divine plan but an accidental product of unconscious process. Finally, George is not as secure as his doctrine sounds because of the trouble he has getting through the day. Late, rushed, and held up by broken cars, snowstorms, and poverty, George is a victim of time and tide, and death, although promising a release from harassment, is a threat to George because his death will leave his family in poverty.

Arising from the problem of time and tide is the question, "*Are you ready to die?*"[10] Strangers speaking with George find themselves "involved, willy-nilly, in a futile but urgent search for the truth,"[11] for an answer to this question. In all his searching George does not find "one of the twelve" (the twelve Olympians of the divine family) who can give him the answer. But there are answers.

The answers to the question of dying correspond to one of the other elements in Updike's work, the mythological and realistic sides of the "romance." Corresponding to the realistic side is the scientific answer suggested by Caldwell's lecture. Life evolves cooperatively and demands from individual members surrender to death:

8. Ibid., p. 63.
9. Ibid., p. 46.
10. Ibid., p. 157.
11. Ibid., p. 83.

. . . the volvox . . . by pioneering this new idea of *coöperation*, rolled life into the kingdom of certain—as opposed to accidental— death. For . . . while each cell is potentially immortal, by volunteering for a specialized function within an organized society of cells, it enters a compromised environment. The strain eventually wears it out and kills it. It dies sacrificially, for the good of the whole.[12]

In other words, man is inevitably caught in a web of death and the only answer to death is submission.

A second answer attempts to restore to life the power of human decision. Here the mythological side of the work reinstates the possibility of noble acts of human will. A way to overcome victimization is to make a great, sacrificial decision to give life for the sake of another. Such a decision is a victory of human will over time and tide and it can, as a victory, be applauded.

The two sides of the romance allow these two answers to stand with independent strength. The use of myth reinstates the world of Chiron, the centaur, and his ability to give life to Prometheus by his sacrificial death. Such a heroic act of will can be applauded, and Chiron is placed in the constellation Sagittarius. The realistic side, epitomized in the obituary, reminds us of a world of pain, frustration, and desperate surrender to death.

A third answer is placed between these two sides, and, because it has neither the mythology nor the realism to support it, it is less clear and constant than the other alternatives. In contrast to the modern scientific and the Greek heroic, this answer has the qualities of an aesthetic form of grace. It is an unexpected answer, and it is suggested in several ways. But it is not an answer which can, like the other two, be established or possessed, and it takes on the qualities of unexpectedness because George in his search wants an answer that is propositional and can be made a possession. He seeks that kind of answer because he wants protection against being watched. Safety posters, Zimmerman the principal, and the God of his "murky" Calvinistic background, intimidate him, and to maintain himself against this external threat he needs some definite an-

12. Ibid., p. 42.

swer. But this third answer is not a possession or a proposition; it cannot be programmed. It dawns on George.

When George and Peter meet the drunkard who asks the important question, *"Are you ready to die?"* George is quick to respond: "What do *you* think the answer is?"[13] But rather than answer, the drunkard turns on the two and accuses George of perverting the boy. George says of him, "That man brought me to my senses. We gotta get you into where it's warm. You're my pride and joy, kid; we gotta guard the silver."[14] The drunkard had directed George's attention away from the search for an answer and brought home to him the fact that standing with him is his son. Wanting to avoid the mistake of the westerners who ignored silver in their frantic search for gold, George realizes that his relation to his son is a precious thing which George, by ignoring it, was perverting. George had seen his son as a reason for not dying; now he sees him as a reason for living.

This answer also comes to George through the memory of his father's words. He remembers walking with his father past a tavern from which they heard laughter. Unlike George, his father was not offended by the laughter and began to insist, *"All joy belongs to the Lord."* George took that "to heart."

> Wherever in the filth and confusion and misery, a soul felt joy, there the Lord came and claimed it as his own; into barrooms and brothels and classrooms and alleys slippery with spittle, no matter how dark and scabbed and remote, in China or Africa or Brazil, wherever a moment of joy was felt, there the Lord stole and added to His enduring domain.[15]

George seems to realize that little things, common joys and laughter, can become what Peter calls, in another context, a Real Presence; that little things have a sacramental potential in which an unexpected answer, an epiphany, can be experienced. Compared to these little joys, "all the rest, all that was not joy, fell away, precipitated, dross that had never been."[16]

The lesson George learned from his father enables him to reach

13. Ibid., p. 158.
14. Ibid., p. 160.
15. Ibid., p. 296.
16. Ibid.

a decision, a decision which gives him another experience of this answer. With the knowledge that he is not sick and will not die, George feels elated. But his elation does not come from his own continued existence; it is due to the fact that around him are little joys, his wife's joy in the land, his father-in-law's joy in the newspaper, his son's joy in the future. George is glad because by living he will be able to sustain these for a while longer. He sees these little joys as opening up to him an "enduring domain."

George's decision to live probably will not end his search for a propositional answer to the problem of death; nor will it end his troubles or his heroic sacrifices. The victory of human will expressed in the mythology and the inevitable victimization by natural process expressed in George's trials and defeats are strong and enduring things. But the decision is still important. At least it suggests that George will experience more of the presence of joy.

Peter's role as narrator allows the work to present Peter's own struggle with the problem of "time and tide." Young Peter finds the present so meager that he lives in the future and dreams of himself as an artist in New York. Thinking it possible to thwart the corroding power of time by locking realities within art and thereby sparing them from change, Peter displays an expansive confidence in his vocational plans, his desire to overcome the dominating quality of natural force by his artistic vocation, to free his future from the troubles that plague his father. His life, an attempt to outwit time and tide, is a Promethean gesture. His dream and ambition are not selfish; his hope is in the future, and he intends by his work to return to his father something of worth.

Peter the boy, moving between dependence on his father and confidence in the future, New York, and art, is contrasted with Peter the man. Since the events of 1947, Peter has been following the Promethean program of his solution to the time-tide dilemma. He has been trying to "stretch" himself "like a large transparent canvas" upon Nature "in the hope that . . . the imprint of a beautiful and useful truth would be taken."[17] This aesthetic vocation, this extended passivity by which change is checked and existence captured, has become, by the time of the narrating, a search

17. Ibid., p. 293.

for an "unsayable" thing. Peter seems dissatisfied with the program consequent to his decision and asks the question, "Was it for this . . . ?" The question rings with an emptiness, a disappointment incongruous with his early optimistic defiance. Now searching for something more, for an "unsayable" thing, Peter turns to the three days; he turns to his father.

Peter's narrative portrait suggests a new relationship growing between himself and the father he remembers. The past becomes a canvas on which the abstraction of a new idea is expressed and on which the Real Presence of his father appears. By telling this story to his mistress, Peter for the first time touches one whom before he never touched, his resurrected father, the quietly joyful man. From his father, from this appearance and presence, Peter receives an answer that is the unsayable thing for which he searched. The ability to apprehend this epiphany is the gift his father gave him with his life.

What Peter the boy projected was a semitranscendent world of art, a world of spirit. This spiritual world provided an escape for Peter from death and sex. The two threats were closely related in his mind: sitting with his girl friend Penny, Peter tells her of his father's possible death while his hand moves as though drawn toward her pelvis; and, tied to the rock, he is plagued by thoughts both of sex's mystery and vulgarity and of his father's death. Death and the physical are threatening to this boy. But the vocation of escape into spirit has not freed him from the threat. He tells the story of his father to his mistress while surrounded by his paintings; he tells it in the presence of sex and death.

Flight is a strong alternative to the mythological and realistic answers to the time-tide question, and it appears to be combined with George's final answer to dying. The figure of the centaur suggests a pull between the earthly and the spiritual, the lofty and the lowly, and George's pains are directly related to that tension. George, too, detests the physical; he hates Nature: "It reminds me of death. All Nature means to me is garbage and confusion and the stink of skunk—*brroo!*"[18] Even the answer suggested by those little joys is cast in an aesthetic mold; for what difference is there

18. Ibid., p. 291.

between these joys which allow all else to "fall away, precipitated, dross that had never been," and those gemlike flames of Walter Pater from which all else, the drift and debris of life, comes to be as though it were not?

George is close to Peter's aestheticism because his religious ideas divorce God from this world. To George, God's mercy "never changes anything at all." God's mercy is infinite only in the sense that it is "at an infinite distance." A world separated from God's concern is a world of death and must be escaped. George only avoids Peter's aestheticism when, unexpectedly, he is brought face-to-face with those offices in his life which humiliate him. He is kept from aesthetic flight by his work, by "the prospect of having again to maneuver among Zimmerman and Mrs. Herzog and all that overbearing unfathomable Olinger gang," by what is called in *Rabbit, Run*, "the *going through* quality of it" [Christianity]. The life of George, a life of accepting death and dying to self, is made possible for him by the ecstatic insight into an enduring domain, an insight given him by the sacramental epiphany of little joys seen in and through his offices, his vocation. Perhaps the power of his resurrected presence imparts the wisdom of that possibility to the narrating Peter, too.

II

The problem of vocation arises from the relation of the personal to the public, the internal to the external, or the psychological to the sociological. Any tension between what a man is and the work he is required to do follows directly the lines of that problem examined in the Introduction, the split between the private and public, or the religious and the nonreligious worlds. It should not be surprising, then, that the question of vocation repeatedly arises in recent fiction or that the frustration that results from a tension between the internal and external lives of characters should so often be associated with the question of vocation. As we saw, the vocational question arises in Powers's work and, in terms of marriage, in De Vries's. It is also found in Malamud's fiction, especially in *The Assistant*. The wider context would include fictions such as *Miss Lonelyhearts*,

Zooey, The Violent Bear It Away, Herzog, Letting Go, and *The Last Gentleman.* And when the question is enlarged to include all consideration of tension between what a person is and what the society wants him to do, the problem of vocation is pervasive.

The problem is acute in Updike's fiction because his narrators and characters are very sensitive, often almost delicate, because they have a strong sense of their individuality or uniqueness, and because they find the world outside of themselves dull, confused, or threatening. They share with Updike his own strong sense of individual importance, the mystery of self; as he puts it in an autobiographical essay: "Why was I I? The arbitrariness of it astounded me; in comparison, nothing was too marvelous."[19] But they find that the worlds in which they live do not support, do not feed, the "I."

At first glance the old people of *The Poorhouse Fair*[20] (1959) seem not to share the problem, since they are rejects from the society. But the fact of their rejection points to the tension between them and the surrounding society, a society which invades them even in their exile. In contrast to Mendelssoln, the former prefect who helped them to accept their positions, young Conner, who, with the other young people in the work, rejects the present and perverts his office because he lusts after something beyond himself, something in the future, oppresses the old folk. In the central ecstatic experience of this montagelike book, Amy Mortis is delivered from the threats around her by recalling Mendelssoln, and the joy imparted by his remembered presence frees Amy and the others from fear of the world's dominion.

The problem of vocation in the stories of *The Same Door*[21] (1959) appears in several forms. One is in the relation of a sensitive boy to the hostile world around him, as in "Friends from Philadelphia," "The Alligators," and "The Happiest I've Been." A second is in the taxing nature of the offices of young husband

---

19. John Updike, *Assorted Prose* (New York: Alfred A. Knopf, 1965), p. 182.
20. John Updike, *The Poorhouse Fair* (New York: Alfred A. Knopf, 1959).
21. John Updike, *The Same Door: Short Stories* (New York: Alfred A. Knopf, 1959).

and father, as in "Toward Evening," "Sunday Teasing," and "Incest." Finally, there are specific vocations and jobs which illuminate the problem, teaching in "Tomorrow and Tomorrow and So Forth" and the artist's life in "A Gift from the City." It is important to note, though, that the pain or uncertainty created by vocation can be, as it is in *The Poorhouse Fair*, a discipline preparing the character for new wisdom or joy. The frustrations of parenthood, for example, are also passages to peace. This interrelationship can be seen in "Ace in the Hole." Here we find a former basketball star who is now a fired used car salesman. In addition he finds his offices as father and husband burdensome; he is tensed by his child's crying and by his wife's criticism. But in the hole Ace begins to dance, and at the end he feels good again.

Although similar to Ace, Harry Angstrom in *Rabbit, Run*[22] (1960) cannot overcome the burdens of his offices as husband, father, and kitchen gadget demonstrator. He cannot because he and his wife, Janice, prefer the childhood their parents force on them to an adulthood which means bearing a pregnancy, coping with a dingy apartment, taking care of a child, and holding down an unchallenging job. When he feels too confined, Rabbit runs, and he seeks out his former basketball coach (no successful husband himself) and a prostitute. He runs to basketball and to sex. Rabbit is joined in his flight by the Reverend Eccles who is an inadequate father to his children, as Lucy his wife says, and no pastor to his flock, as Kruppenbach, the fierce Lutheran, points out. Unable to see his offices as supportive of his inner needs and desires, Rabbit runs to break loose, as he once did on the basketball floor. But the basketball model is inadequate, since in a basketball game Rabbit could get free from opponents who were human and identifiable. The enemy of his adult life is not human or limited; it is poverty, boredom, a series of meaningless jobs, and a sloppy wife. Sex also serves as a model taken from his earlier life, but it too is inadequate. Sex entangles him in the lives of two women through conception, birth, and child-raising. Harry develops, as the narrator says, "no taste for the dark, tangled visceral aspect of Christianity,

22. John Updike, *Rabbit, Run* (New York: Alfred A. Knopf, 1960).

the *going through* quality of it."[23] He is a luminous figure who wants to soar over life and drop his seeds of joy whenever he can. The problem is that the soaring and the dropping spread unhappiness and death. What he experiences, then, is the need to be a successful husband and father and his inability to be one. His responsibilities are too deadening and his basketball and sex memories are too lovely to allow him a sense of fulfillment in the discipline of *"going through."*

The problem of vocation in *Pigeon Feathers and Other Stories*[24] (1962), is largely formulated in terms of the artist's calling. The artist relates himself to his exterior world by recalling or doing justice to the beauty of former things. By recalling these things the artist gives them life and is refreshed by them. Remembering and forgetting are linked, as they are at other points in the Updike corpus, with living and dying. As the narrator says in the triptych, "The Blessed Man of Boston, My Grandmother's Thimble, and Fanning Island," "O Lord, bless these poor paragraphs, that would do in their vile ignorance Your work of resurrection."[25] Like sacraments, refreshing memories are only granted when the mind is worthy, as in "Walter Briggs," and memories bring refreshment or freedom from guilt, as in "The Persistence of Desire." Consequently, a particular from the past is an almost sacred datum which cannot be altered, as skunks cannot be altered in "Should Wizard Hit Mommy?"

While particulars in the worlds of his sensitive characters can support and refresh them, generally their worlds bewilder them. As it is put in "The Astronomer," "What is the past, after all, but a vast sheet of darkness in which a few moments, pricked at random, shine?" The general situation is antagonistic to the individual, as it is to the young boys in "You'll Never Know, Dear, How Much I Love You" and "A Sense of Shelter." The general character of the world as dark or threatening heightens the value of remembered moments. In order to be an artist, the one who recalls

23. Ibid., p. 237.
24. John Updike, *Pigeon Feathers and Other Stories* (New York: Alfred A. Knopf, 1962).
25. Ibid., p. 299.

must be free from his environment, as Allen Dow must be free
even from his mother in "Flight."

The contrast these characters feel between a general exterior
situation that threatens them and isolated moments which bear
healing powers is revealed in "Pigeon Feathers" and in the triptych from which I already have quoted. In the first, David's world
turns dark as he cannot find an adequate answer in it to the question of dying. But when he buries the pigeons he has shot he is
arrested by the beauty of their wings. This potent detail delivers
him from the general threat. The narrator of the triptych has almost
been overcome by a menace constituted of people with whom he
must live and work. Returning to his home in Pennsylvania, he is
delivered from the threat by remembering, as he contemplates her
thimble, the unique life of his grandmother. Similarly, when the
narrator of "Packed Dirt, Churchgoing, A Dying Cat, A Traded
Car" goes home to visit his sick father, he leaves behind him a
deadening life of work and partying, and he is revived by the stout
eccentricities of this dying man.

The vocation of the artist as well as the offices of father and
husband are no less significant for the novel *Of the Farm*[26] (1965).
When Joey Robinson comes home to visit his dying mother, he
returns as a recently divorced and remarried advertising specialist.
Joey realizes how much that was of value has slipped away from
his life when it is juxtaposed to his origins. He encounters the integrity and trustfulness of his mother and his own poetic youth. This
juxtaposition evokes from him the poetic language in which the
story is narrated. But Joey, as a reborn artist, does not, in the
pastor's words, "Aerate[s] the barren density of brute matter with
the penetrations of the mind, of the spirit!"[27] He, like Rabbit, lacks
the "*going through*" ability. Compared to his mother, Joey is precious, standing above his world and his wife, quickening them with
his words. Although he reclaims as an artist some healing memories,
the presence of his dead father and his youthful self, it is the life of
particular people around him, his wife and mother, and the value of
his memories from which the strength of his narration is derived.

26. John Updike, *Of the Farm* (New York: Alfred A. Knopf, 1965).
27. Ibid., p. 151.

THE PROBLEM OF VOCATION

The presence of people who can accept their own dying and who, although humiliated by their positions and offices, are joyful, balances those characters in the Updike corpus who have been victimized by a society unable to provide them with a meaningful position or job. These suffering but joyful people represent what the minister of *Of the Farm* calls "the concrete reality of Christ." When Updike allows his resurrected characters, from Mendelssoln to Mrs. Robinson, to speak for themselves, he is a writer who, although expansively conscious of the creative power of fictional language, as conscious as some of his characters and narrators are, expresses his vocational debt to people who lived and died in offices.

In his next two books, *The Music School*[28] (1966) and *Couples*[29] (1968), we find Updike in transition. Although a few of the stories collected in *The Music School* go back to youth and the early years of marriage, Updike spends most of his time in both books with the bitter dregs of marriage on the rocks.[30]

The characters in the short stories are often lonely and at odds with their worlds, as in "The Dark," "The Morning," "The Hermit," "At a Bar in Charlotte Amalie," "The Family Meadow," and "The Bulgarian Poetess." Loneliness is mixed with marital troubles in "Leaves," "The Stare," "Avec La Bébé-sitter," "Twin Beds in Rome," "My Lover Has Dirty Fingernails," "The Rescue," and "The Music School." Loneliness and marital difficulties seem to be the result of the move Updike's fiction makes from eastern Pennsylvania and youth to New England and Dante's "mid-point" in life.

The sense of disappointment in troubled marriage seems symptomatic of the experience in the Dantesque woods, loneliness and despair. This seems clear from *Couples*. As with De Vries, the death of marriage and communication is a sign of spiritual distress. These losses aggravate the problem which vocation can become in a rapidly changing world, and it is not surprising that in this book

28. John Updike, *The Music School* (New York: Alfred A. Knopf, 1966).
29. John Updike, *Couples* (New York: Alfred A. Knopf, 1968).
30. I know that phrase is somewhere in De Vries—at least it should be.

Piet Hanema, who, incidentally, could walk into a De Vries novel without scrambling a line, is losing his job as well as his wife.

The world exterior to Piet is primarily a group of people who are several stages farther away from a religiously ordered life than he. Ringleader for the group is Freddy Thorne who goads the couples into playing games with confession and intimacy: Expressions, Truth, Wonderful, and the four-handed game to which it all finally leads, mate-swapping. These indoor sadomasochistic sports form attractive alternatives to the emptiness and boredom experienced by these couples in their daily offices.

If Piet were doing well in his marriage and job he would not need what these other people have to offer. But he no longer can do the kind of carpentry which he enjoys; his wife does not share his interest in sex and religion; and Piet gets his mistress Foxy pregnant. Piet is a failure in all his offices. He is not an adequate son, since he blames himself for his parents' death; his work slips away from him; he has no close relation to his daughters; and he fails as a husband. Given these failures and judging from Updike's other works, I think it is safe to say that, although Piet's divorce has a healing effect, this healing is not permanent; for the convincing rebirths in Updike's fiction occur not by changing jobs but by being changed within one's offices. Meaningful changes occur when a person is able to accept the death to his self-interest and the awakening of new life effected in him by the law and grace of vocation.

III

Vocation constitutes a problem for most of Updike's characters, and this problem can be clarified by a fuller look at the Lutheran understanding of vocation which seems to have influenced the position the problem has in Updike's fiction. We should look, then, at Luther's attempt to rescue daily work from meaninglessness.[31]

31. Cf. Martin Luther, "The Freedom of a Christian" and "A Commentary on St. Paul's Epistle to the Galatians" in *Martin Luther: Selections From His Writings,* ed. John Dillenberger (Garden City: Doubleday and Co., Inc., 1961).

Luther's stand on the question of vocation is a deeply theocentric one. God is so high that human distinctions, including the medieval distinction between religious and ordinary work, are unimportant to him, and God is so holy that the possibility of achieving a level of righteousness in a religious vocation which surpasses the level of ordinary people is not one he recognizes. Under the gaze of God, the *coram Deo*, all human distinctions are neutralized.[32]

The gaze of God was not for Luther first of all the protective watchfulness of God. Rather, it was that presence of God which can only disconcert a man, only threaten him. Under the *coram Deo*, a man feels that everything is wrong with him, everything is hostile. As Ernest Gordon Rupp says in *The Righteousness of God*:

> Thus the sinner is hemmed in with anxiety and fear, and his conscience is a prison to him. Cramped, cabined, and confined in a kind of spiritual claustrophobia, the experience passes over into its opposite, the restless desire to flee to the ends of the earth, under the desperate certainty that there can be no escape from God.[33]

Escaping God becomes an obsession for such a man because this gaze is such a constant intimidation. Perhaps a better word than intimidation is humiliation. Humility is a sense of personal unworthiness and not simply a gentlemanly virtue; it is a painful awareness of personal vulnerability under God's gaze.

We need not rehearse all of Updike's works to see how important to them is this feeling of vulnerability. It is most fully a part of George Caldwell's consciousness in *The Centaur*, for he is a man who feels watched all the time and senses the constant presence of death. Along with other characters in the Updike corpus, George's life is marked by humiliation, vulnerability, and a fear of death.

---

32. Of the interpretations of Luther's thought, I found the following to be most helpful: Robert H. Fife, *Young Luther: The Intellectual and Religious Development of Martin Luther to 1518* (New York: Macmillan Co., 1928), Ernest Gordon Rupp, *Luther's Progress to the Diet of Worms: 1521* (Chicago: Wilcox and Follett Co., 1951) and *The Righteousness of God: Luther Studies* (New York: Philosophical Library, 1953), Heinrich Bornkamm, *Luther's World of Thought*, trans. Martin Bertram (St. Louis: Concordia Publishing House, 1958), and Philip S. Watson, *Let God be God* (London: Epworth Press, 1947).

33. Rupp, *The Righteousness of God: Luther Studies*, p. 109.

A second point important to Luther's doctrine of vocation is his understanding of the righteousness of God. The change in Luther's theological thought, which seems to have pointed him in the direction that finally led to his break from Rome, came about by his work with Paul's Letter to the Romans. In the first chapter Paul speaks of God's righteousness, and Luther at first took this to mean the righteousness of God which clarified how separate God is from men, how, in distinction, unrighteous men are. But then he saw that this righteousness was God's gift to men. When a man is humiliated by the righteousness of God, when he is intimidated by God's gaze, then righteousness is imputed to him as God's gift, and righteousness becomes grace.[34]

The gift of God's righteousness is not, Luther thought, isolated from the normal experiences which come to a man. Luther calls the things we see and hear the masks and veils of God's presence, a presence which confronts men first as law and then as grace. Of course, for Luther Christ is the primary and essential mask or veil of God in whom men confront the divine presence first in judgment but then also in grace. But once a man confronts God's law and grace in Christ, he meets God's presence in other moments of experience, too.[35]

Characters in Updike's fiction often experience an uplifting sense of joy in and through the ordinary things and events of life. Although we do not find his characters confronting Christ and undergoing judgment and grace in that confrontation in an explicitly Christian way, the pattern described by Luther is followed by several of Updike's characters even though Luther's christocentric emphasis is gone. The "enduring domain" of the Lord, as it is put in *The Centaur*, is opened up on several occasions. David in "Pigeon Feathers" is delivered from his fear of death by the epiphany of aesthetic fullness which reveals to him the presence of a Creator who will also sustain David's life. In *The Poorhouse Fair* the inmates are granted a joy in the resurrection from death as they confront eternal life in the mask or veil of Mendelssoln's persistent

34. Cf. Martin Luther, *Lectures on Romans,* trans. and ed. with introduction and notes by Wilhelm Pauck (Philadelphia: Westminster Press, 1961).
35. Cf. Watson, *Let God be God,* pp. 115–16.

presence. And George Caldwell is drawn out of his fear and intimidation when he is given a share in the joy which "belongs to the Lord." Indeed, Updike's fiction itself often arises from and conveys the experience of confronting in a particular mask or veil the fullness of enduring life. The act of recall, which lies so close to resurrection in his fiction, is an act of doing justice to a particular which, when fully apprehended, grants the viewer a full peace. His fiction is often offered as a sacrament in which the power to resist nonexistence and forgetfulness is veiled. A firm sense of resurrection, expressed in his poem "Seven Stanzas at Easter," seems to underlie his work.

Given the theocentric and christocentric points of Luther's thought, the *coram Deo*, and the presence of God in masks and veils, we are able to understand Luther's view of human work. Certainly human work cannot be for him man's contribution to his own salvation. First of all, a man is called to work in darkness, to respond to the needs of his neighbors, for example, not because such work is uplifting to him but because in his office a man is called on to spend himself. A man learns in his daily work first of all what it means to die. Vocation is a cross on which a man's old, human nature, his desire to preserve and extend himself, must perish.[36] In contrast to the doctrine of vocation in the monastic system from which Luther turned, his own view of vocation saw a Christian called on to labor not in order to become more holy but in order to die. But in that dying, in the sacrifice of work, the event of resurrection, the gift of God's righteousness, and the gift of faith, break out. If a man does not succumb to the temptation of fleeing his own death, he is raised in his office to a new life.

Many of Updike's characters, Conner and his wards, Rabbit and Eccles, George and Peter, Joey Robinson, and others, are called on to spend themselves in offices and jobs which they are tempted to resist. These people struggle between the alternatives of, on the one hand, accepting their places in life with consequent humiliation and even death, and, on the other, rejecting their positions and striving to secure, by their own spiritual effort or fantasy, some

36. Cf. Gustef Wingren, *Luther on Vocation*, trans. Carl C. Rasmussen (Philadelphia: Muhlenberg Press, 1957), pp. 30-60.

sense of escape or salvation. Only some of his characters, such as Amy Mortis, George, and Mrs. Robinson, can accept the dying that comes with their positions in life. But more subtly, several of the young parents in Updike's stories are people who are dying to their own interests and resurrected to new joys. Young mothers spend themselves in caring for demanding children, and young husbands share an unusual amount of the familial burdens. Marriage itself is a kind of cross. That point is secured by "Giving Blood" in *The Music School*; the blood which Richard and Joan Maple donate parallels the common sacrifice they must make of their own self-interest in order for their marriage to go on. This couple and other characters in his fiction are raised to new strength and peace when they accept the burdens of the offices in which they stand. The clearest of these is George. He finds his positions as father, husband, and teacher irksome when they bring him pain and prevent him from carrying on his quest for an answer to dying. But at crucial points, George is able to accept his offices, and when he does he receives a new courage and joy.

What Updike seems to take from Luther, then, is a sacramental understanding of work. Work is deadening; work has no direct relation to the religion of grace. But in, through, and under work a man can receive the presence of God first in judgment but then also in grace.

The religious understanding of work can be clarified further if we look for a moment at those characteristics of the world of primitive and ancient people which tend to make work in that world meaningful. For one thing, acts were meaningful for such people because performance was rehearsal, the repetitions of the performance by a divine figure or a great hero of the past. There is no break for these people, then, between religious and profane activities. Every act for such people is done under a paradigm, and the act is raised to religious significance because it is at the same time an act of imitation, of devotion.[37]

Work is no problem for a primitive or ancient people also because each individual understands himself as contributing to a

37. Cf. Mircea Eliade, *Cosmos and History: The Myth of the Eternal Return* (New York: Harper and Row, 1959), p. 28.

significant community, a community which has an existence and an identity that precede and transcend each individual. Since he looks to the community as primary, the individual has no anxiety about what kind of work he ought to do or why he is employed as he is. The center of will and power was not in the individual but in the community, and full admission into the community delivered a man from the deathlike threat of individuality or exile.[38]

Finally, work was no problem for primitive and ancient man because the natural world was not an alien or hostile "it." Human decision and work did not form an insular and precious point of will in a sea of cold and unthinking matter.

> The fundamental difference between the attitudes of modern and ancient man as regards the surrounding world is this: for modern, scientific man the phenomenal world is primarily an "It"; for ancient—and also for primitive—man it is a "Thou."[39]

A man's work has significance because it is a response not to a dead or hostile world but to a world filled with life and meaning.

Anthropologists and historians of religion have made us aware, therefore, of the problem work is for modern man, since he has no crowd of active, memorable examples under which to work, since he is a member of no all-embracing and enduring community, and since the world around him is a movement of unconscious forces and unwilled effects. Aggravating the problem for the modern Christian or Jew is the fact that these religious traditions speak more easily about human need and human death than about human will and work.

An effect of a preoccupation with grace is the neutralization of the natural world; preoccupation with grace involves an almost exclusive attention to personal relationships. Yahweh is presented in the Bible as being in conflict, or working with, not the material world but with Israel, as having intercourse not with the ground but with his people. The creation of Yahweh which is of primary

38. Cf. Gerhard von Rad, *Old Testament Theology,* trans. P. M. G. Stalker (New York: Harper and Brothers, 1962), p. 37.
39. H. and H. A. Frankfort, "Myth and Reality" in *Before Philosophy: The Intellectual Adventure of Ancient Man* (Baltimore: Penguin Books, 1949), p. 12.

concern for Israel is the creation of the people, and the general creation or the creation of a holy land form only the background or the stage for the personal struggle and communion Yahweh carries on with his uniquely created and destined people. Certainly Israel always understood the world as created by a free decision of God as much as Israel herself was so created. But the emphasis for a religion of grace is the exclusiveness and priority of the divine decision to save. The "natural" world is not as significant religiously for Israel as it is for primitive and other ancient peoples, and that neutralization of the "natural" world magnifies the problem of meaningful work for Judaism and Christianity.

The second component that contributes to meaningful work in a primitive's life, we saw, was the priority of the community in which stories about work were preserved and in which work was commissioned and the fruit of work shared. Community is important in the Bible too, but the sense of community in Israel does not aid the problem of work because the community of Israel is a reservoir or channel of grace. Vocation for Israel was election, its calling to stand in a unique and purposeful relationship with Yahweh, its calling to be malleable to Yahweh's gracious designs. Although the divine permeated all of Israel's time and space and a worker knew that those who build a house labor in vain unless the Lord builds it (Psalm 127), the overriding and preeminent character of Israel's soteriological identity and destiny meant a deemphasis of work and the natural world, and the nature of the community as one created by and for the purposes of grace meant that the works of men's hands, such as agriculture and the construction of cities if they were not evil, as the prophets at times seem to imply, were questionable or, at best, unimportant.

The final component essential to meaningful work in a primitive's world is the crowd of heroes and divine workmen who provide the workman with paradigms and whose power is reexpressed in the world by the workman's efforts. A crowd of such paradigms Israel lacked. This lack may explain the ease with which Israel, especially the northern agricultural population, went over to Baal worship. A fertility religion of this kind gave the northern farmer a set of divine figures whose activity his own planting expressed. It is also not surprising that the form of life most typical of the Israelites, one to which the prophets so often recalled the people, namely a seminomadic form, is one calling for very few human skills. It demands no houses, no planting, and few tools. It is not a way of life in which archetypes for human activity are very necessary.

Moving to the New Testament we can see that these three emphases are enlarged. In the highly apocalyptic world of the New Testament the present world and the present age are under judgment, and attention is taken from them and shifted to the concluding activity of God which has begun in the coming, death, and resurrection of Jesus and will be finished in his imminent return. Surely, Jesus knew something about carpentry and fishing and Paul knew enough about tentmaking and sailing to make a living of one and to give advice on the other. But such matters are neutral incidentals, and one could hardly suggest that Jesus' advice to cast from the other side of the boat made the early church's fishing trips more meaningful or successful. Also, the community of the New Testament was more sharply focused than was Israel on the soteriological intentions of God. The calling of the Christian was a calling away from his nets, away from plowing and burying the dead, into the community of grace. Vocation is an election into the fellowship of the new Israel, the community of the new age, and the work of a Christian was to overcome in his own life that which resisted the presence of God and to bear witness in the world to the church. Finally Christianity does not provide the church with a crowd of great or divine workers. Who knows how good a carpenter Jesus was? And when Christians made tents, they did not do so as a way of bringing Paul the worker into their worlds once more. It is not very surprising that in the history of Christianity an array of saints and patrons who have particular meaning for separate activities and offices in human life should develop. Although these saints and patrons were not themselves always such great creators or exemplars of the kind of office or work of which they are patrons, at least they touch those points of human life with a compassionate and empowering care whose ultimate source is divine.

Since the components which provide a religious significance for daily work are not ensured by the Bible, we can expect that in the development of Christian life and thought, vocation should be thought of as a religious calling that brings a man out of the world and into a monastery or into the clergy. This separation of religious vocation from ordinary work had the advantage of retaining the radical dissociation from the world which the call to discipleship, perhaps most fully articulated in the Sermon on the Mount, makes plain. Perhaps the thought of Luther and Calvin, which tried to destroy the medieval distinction, was not able to retain the purity of divine vocation which, at its best moments, the monastic movement protected.[40] As Karl Barth says:

> Protestantism successfully expelled monasticism by recalling the fact that κλῆσις is the presupposition of all Christian existence. But it lost sight of the divine grandeur and purity of this κλῆσις, which were always in some sense retained by monasticism. . . . Its Scylla was the concealed but later more blatant secularism of its concept of calling—a secularism which was unavoidable from the very outset.[41]

It is especially with Martin Luther's name that the attempt to overcome the separation of religious from ordinary work is to be identified. It is, as we have seen, this Lutheran view of work that has most deeply influenced John Updike.

Updike's fiction is representative of the tension between the individual and his offices which generally marks recent literature not so much when he presents a character like George Caldwell as when people like Harry Angstrom, Peter Caldwell, and Joey Robinson take the stage. These characters do not see their lives quickened by a new life graciously given in and through office. If anything, such quickening will result from their ability to express in their lives something of the exalted acts of Prometheus, Uranus, or

---

40. The following are helpful studies in the problem of vocation for the New Testament and the Christian church: Paul S. Minear, "Work and Vocation in Scripture" in *Work and Vocation: A Christian Discussion*, ed. John Nelson (New York: Harper and Brothers, 1954), Donald R. Heiges, *The Christian's Calling* (Philadelphia: Muhlenberg Press, 1958), Alan Richardson, *The Biblical Doctrine of Work* (London: SCM Press, 1952), W. A. Beardslee, *Human Achievement and Divine Vocation in the Message of Paul* (London: SCM Press, 1961), and Karl Barth, *Church Dogmatics*, Vol. III/4, trans. A. T. Macckay et al. (Edinburgh: T. and T. Clark, 1961), esp. pp. 601–5.
41. Karl Barth, *Church Dogmatics*, Vol. III/4, p. 602.

Icarus. These models of self-sufficiency, self-expansion, and flight are alternatives to *"going through"* which are supported by those among Updike's narrators who view their world as dead or dying and who redeem particulars from oblivion through the power of their uplifting words. While such characters and narrators seem precious at times or dependent upon the supporting ground of sacrificial parents, they provide an alternative which, while put under pressure, emerges as dominant.

It appears that in our time, for reasons suggested in the Introduction, the affirmation of one's offices is very perplexing. Whether the problem lies in the society or in the individual, the Lutheran call to celebrate daily work as a spiritual discipline becomes increasingly difficult to answer.

As in De Vries, then, we find in Updike a painful separation between a remembered world of spiritual possibilities and a present world of discouraging realities. This split between the self and the society is a problem of such magnitude that it moves beyond the covers of the artist's books and threatens the vocation of the artist himself. The strain of separation appears both in the way Updike places on his Jewish scapegoat, Bech,[42] the principal anxiety of the writer's vocation, the prospect of running dry within a decade, and in his heralded[43] return to the net of his eastern Pennsylvania starting point.

42. John Updike, *Bech: A Book* (New York: Alfred A. Knopf, 1970).
43. John Updike, "Pop, Mom, Moon," *The Atlantic,* August 1971, pp. 48–63 and "Rabbit's Evening Out," *Esquire,* September 1971, pp. 109–12, 191–92, 194, and 196.

4.

The Fixer and the
Death of God

The problems for religious thought and life suggested by the Nietz-schean phrase "the death of God" were somewhat obscured, per-haps, in those widely publicized discussions of the sixties, by the personalities and the rhetoric of the "death of God" school. Those problems, however, are not limited to some individuals or to a very brief chapter in current theological debate. In fact, they are not even limited to the modern period, although they seem to have been increasingly felt in this century and have formed a major crisis for religious thought in this country during the last twenty years. The crisis suggested by the phrase has made itself felt in recent fiction, too, particularly in fiction concerned with religious matters, and theological critics such as Nathan A. Scott, Charles I. Glicksberg, and Gabriel Vahanian have convincingly pointed out how central to the literary imagination the "death of God" in our time has been.

The question suggested by the phrase is this: Are there moments in human life when the word "God" cannot be used with a sense of its appropriateness or meaningfulness? The answer to that question is affirmative, and there appear to be three moments when the word "God" lacks meaning and appropriateness: the nonreligious, public domain which a pluralistically religious society created for itself, a society described in the Introduction; moments of gratuitous suf-fering, that is, moments which contradict human expectations, de-sires, or needs; and moments which conform rather totally to human intentions, predictions, or desires. As in the fiction of the other writers we are studying and in the works of other recent American authors, use of the word "God" is rendered questionable in moments of all three kinds. The fiction of Malamud includes these several kinds too, but the moment of human experience upon which *The Fixer* centers is the loss of God in the midst of gratuitous human suffering.

As William Styron used a particular historical instance and an identifiable group to expose the general occasion for and consequences of revolution in *The Confessions of Nat Turner*, Malamud took an actual occurrence as the basis for his novel in order to root it in reality and then to move from one set of events to a general revelation of God's "death" as a contemporary fact. The actual occurrence is the case of Mendel Beiliss, a case described by a book which appeared in the same year as *The Fixer*, Maurice Samuel's *Blood Accusation*.[1] Samuel dwells on the setting of the case, the anti-Semitism of late Tsarist Russia, the bizarre characters involved in the process, and the response of the Western press to the affair. The trial of Beiliss began in September 1913, almost three years after Beiliss had been arrested for allegedly stabbing a Christian boy numerous times, and, difficult as it may be to believe, Beiliss was thought by the populace and by some officials to have murdered the boy ritualistically, as part of some Jewish practice of using blood for magical matzos.

Malamud's primary interest is not in writing historical fiction, and he does little to convey to us a feeling for what this period, area, or event really were like. Rather, he takes the historical event and frees his character from it in order to focus not on the external matters, historical or sociological, but on internal struggles. From Mendel Beiliss, the thirty-nine-year-old father of five children, Malamud creates Yakov Bok, thirty, childless, deserted by his wife, and disillusioned as a pilgrim. From the public figure and event we are given a deeply introspective and, at points, confessional fiction.

1. Maurice Samuel, *Blood Accusation: The Strange History of the Beiliss Case* (New York: Alfred A. Knopf, 1966). Cf. also Mendel Beiliss, *The Story of My Sufferings*, trans. Harrison Goldberg with introductions by Herman Bernstein and Arnold Margolin (New York: Mendel Beiliss Publishing Co., 1926).

THE FIXER

I

The work begins with a cyclical prelude, and it opens at the moment the body of the boy is discovered and the charge of ritual murder is aired. Yakov Bok becomes uneasy when he hears of these events, for he does not feel at home in Kiev, he recalls the pogroms which terrified his youth, and he knows that he resides in a district of Kiev in which Jews are forbidden to live.

In this prelude we go back with Bok almost half a year, to the point where he leaves the shtetl as a pilgrim to holy, prosperous Kiev. Bok sees only the unfortunate side of shtetl life, the poverty, the lack of innovation, and the absence of God during pogroms: "He's with us till the Cossacks come galloping, then he's elsewhere. He's in the outhouse, that's where he is."[2] Bok is weary of the social and religious existence provided by the shtetl: "He [God] doesn't see us and he doesn't care. Today I want my piece of bread, not in Paradise."[3] Since he considers Kiev a more promising center of life, he sets out on his journey.

On his way toward "Holy Kiev, mother of Russian cities,"[4] Bok lets a Christian pilgrim, an old woman, ride with him on his wagon, but she and Bok share nothing; when the wagon breaks down, Bok is again alone. This could be a warning that Bok's pilgrimage is ill-advised, but he persists, even when, as he crosses the river to Kiev, he hears the boatman curse Jews. Rather than resist this vicious appraisal of his people, Bok drops the holy prayer things, which Shmuel had given him, into the river.

In Kiev, "Jerusalem of Russia,"[5] Bok becomes one of a group of Christian pilgrims visiting the graves of saints, but he cannot exchange his Jewish identity for a Christian one so quickly and easily. He takes up residence in the Jewish quarter and begins a set of acts by which his Jewishness can be more gradually destroyed. The opportunity to reject Jewishness is given Bok when he

---

2. Bernard Malamud, *The Fixer* (New York: Farrar, Straus and Giroux, 1966), p. 12.

3. Ibid., p. 17.

4. Ibid., p. 20.

5. Ibid., p. 29.

comes under the favor of Nikolai Maximovitch Lebedev and his daughter Zinaida. When Nikolai employs Bok, first in his home and then in his brickworks, Bok must falsify his name and origins because Nikolai belongs to an anti-Semitic organization. Bok is a pilgrim seeking money, and he is seduced into the unclean paradise at the expense of his Jewish identity. However, when Zinaida offers herself to the pilgrim during her menstrual period, Bok seems to recognize where he is and runs.

Bok's anxiety is caused by a Jewish identity which he cannot escape. Everything reminds him that he is living falsely. He reads newspapers, Russian history, and Spinoza, and all three make him aware that, by hiding his Jewish identity, he has withdrawn from life, from history. Newspaper stories are frightening, the history of Russia is not his own, and the God of the nontraditional Spinoza is only a thin abstraction.[6]

Bok is rudely drawn into history when he is arrested, identified as a Jew, victimized by the history of Russian anti-Semitism, and publicized in the newspapers. More, he becomes the unwilling epitome of history, an example for the Russians of Jewish religious fanaticism.

After this cyclical prelude, the plot begins, and it has three parts. The first, including chapters three through five, presents Bok's resistance to the charge and his belief that he will soon be vindicated. The second, including chapters six and seven, renders Bok as without hope in any human assistance or legal justice and as wrestling with religious answers to his plight. The third, chapters eight and nine, reveals his decision to be a man and a Jew in his situation. The prelude is integral to the plot in that it stands in relation to the real pilgrimage upon which Bok embarks once he enters prison, the pilgrimage to his identity as a Jew and as a man.

Bok's hope in a speedy vindication during the first part of the plot is centered on B. A. Bibikov, the somewhat optimistic humanist and rationalist who puts his confidence in government and law. Bibikov underestimates evil, the range and profundity of anti-Semitism, and he assures Bok that the charge and the penalty will

6. Ibid., p. 70.

be minor. Though pleasant, Bibikov's optimism, his confidence in the rationality of political and legal procedures, is ungrounded. It looks weak as the feeling against Bok, expressed by irrational men, mounts.

Irrational, vicious anti-Semitism is expressed against Bok by the depositions of Nikolai and Zinaida, by the prosecuting attorney, Grubeshov, who pulls questions for Bok out of a fund of murky, distorted notions of Jewish offices and practices, and by Father Anastasy, a "specialist" on Jewish life and belief. Marta Golov,[7] who is linked in Bibikov's mind with a gang of thieves and with the murder of her son, is, in contrast, remade into a devout and afflicted Christian saint. Surrounding the insecure walls of Bibikov's rationally founded city of law is a hoard of hateful and superstitious powers.

Bok senses where the real power lies. He feels caught in a net of accusations and judgments over which he has no control: "Being born a Jew meant being vulnerable to history, including its worst errors."[8] Against the rising swell of irrationality around him and the increasing anxiety within, Bibikov's reassurances are weak. Although sudden, Bibikov's death is not surprising.

In the second part Bok feels dead, his hope all gone. "For weeks he had lived with this potential savior in his thoughts, this just and gentle man; depended on him somehow to free him from prison, the trap laid for him, from the crime itself, the horrifying accusation."[9] Corresponding to his rising spiritual torment are his physical pains, infected feet, asthmatic attacks, and food poisoning. In addition, the officials humiliate him with minute searches of his naked body, first twice and then three times each day.

Bok is under such pressure from his afflictions that the narrator allows the point of view to shift at several moments from the third person to the first. In this confessional context and under these

7. Malamud has combined the two mothers of the actual Beiliss case. The mother of the murdered boy seems to have been quite free of blame. It was the mother of the boy's friend, Vera Cheberyak, who ran a house for thieves and lived with her blinded lover.
8. Malamud, *The Fixer*, p. 155.
9. Ibid., p. 182.

heavy pressures, Bok's preoccupation with religion arises to replace the preoccupation with freedom expressed in the first part.

Bok's concern with religion shifts his interest from Spinoza's philosophical speculation about God's relation to history to Bok's own biblical understanding that God acts in history. Turning primarily to the Psalms, he recalls bits of lyrics written by and for a people in darkness, a people undergoing deathlike experiences similar to his own. The bits he remembers come initially from laments, the sixth, seventh, tenth, thirty-fifth, and one hundred and second Psalms, although he does not seem to recall even more poignant and distressed cries from these and other psalms. The list ends with a part of Psalm 18 which Bok renders ironically. The writer of the Psalm is celebrating delivery by God from enemies, but unlike the ancient king, Bok does not feel that God is fighting on his side. God can more easily be thought of by Bok as fighting not the enemies but Bok himself.

The pain of the struggle is aggravated for Bok by false motions toward delivery. When taken to the courthouse to receive his indictment, he is only urged to confess. In addition, he hears an irrational tirade on the oppression of Russia by the Jews. Bok quickly finds himself back in his solitary cell, and he is sick of being a Jew, "sick of their history, destiny, blood guilt."[10]

As part of his struggle with religious ideas, Bok is given a set of phylacteries and a prayer shawl. When the guard takes these away, Bok is given a New Testament which he reads. He is moved by the passion story, especially by the moment in which "Jesus cried out help to God but God gave no help. There was a man crying out in anguish in the dark, but God was on the other side of his mountain."[11] Bok is also intrigued by the Beatitudes, and he memorizes them.

Prepared for the church by the Beatitudes and passion of Jesus, Bok can only be repelled by the church when it makes its appearance to his cell in the person of a priest. The priest is interested in bribing Bok into conversion with the prospect that this would effect

10. Ibid., p. 227.
11. Ibid., p. 232.

his release from prison. The contrast between the religious attitudes of Jesus and the Christianity epitomized by the priest, an attitude of antipathy against Jews, is torturous to Bok.

Bok moves from the Christian to the Jewish Scriptures when he is given some pages from the Old Testament. Unable to appreciate the story of God's acts in Hebrew history, Bok is fascinated by the Bible's description of human suffering and achievement. In contrast to suffering humanity, God appears inferior.

> The purpose of the covenant, Yakov thinks, is to create human experience, although human experience baffles God. God is after all God; what he is is what he is: God. What does he know about such things? Has he ever worshipped God? Has he ever suffered? How much, after all, has he experienced? God envies the Jews: it's a rich life. Maybe he would like to be human, it's possible, nobody knows. That's this God, Yahweh, the one who appears out of clouds, cyclones, burning bushes; talking.[12]

Compared to Bok's suffering in the complex net of Jewish-Russian history, God's life, divorced from history as it appears to be, looks pale and effete. Rather than point him to God, then, the experiences and work of a prophet like Hosea serve to illuminate for Bok the suffering which marks his own and his people's history.

Finally, the religious nature of this middle part is amplified by the visit to Bok's cell of Shmuel, his father-in-law, and their conversation about God. Like the friends of Job, Shmuel tells Bok that the cause of his plight is Bok's separation from God. God is indispensable to a Jew's life, he insists, and without the covenant Jews would have disappeared long ago. But Bok does not feel that he has forsaken God; God, instead, has abandoned him. "I blame him for not existing. Or if he does it's on the moon or stars but not here."[13] Bok concludes, "He's [God is] a cold wind and try and keep warm. To tell the truth, I've written him off as a dead loss."[14]

With his conclusion that God is gone and that Jewish covenant theology has no meaning when history is so barren of God's pres-

12. Ibid., p. 240.
13. Ibid., p. 256.
14. Ibid., pp. 257–58.

ence, Bok ends his religious ruminations. For Bok, the only reality is his own experience of pain and injustice.

In the third part Bok's sufferings increase, but he wills to become a Jewish man, not in a religious way but as a mode of self-affirmation and as an act of charity. His suffering is increased when he is chained to the wall and searched six times a day because Shmuel's visit was discovered, and he becomes a Jewish man by claiming his wife's illegitimate son as his own and by holding out against the officials for a fair trial.

Bok decides that the Jews are a people in which he can believe; they have done nothing to cancel their right to exist as a people, and, given the absence of God, Bok makes a covenant of his own with this people. He will do for them what he can. As part of this covenant Bok refuses to give in to the temptations offered him by the officials' bribes. When his wife visits him, Bok is given the opportunity to affirm his Jewish identity, by giving her child his name.

Finally, after more than two years, the machinery of law begins to move, and Bok receives his indictment and a lawyer. Both confirm Bok's new identity as a Jewish man, for the lawyer tells him, "You suffer for us all . . . ,"[15] and the indictment is heavy with blood accusation.

Bok realizes that to be a Jew is to be in history. As a non-Jew in the brickyard he had tried to escape history; now he is enmeshed in it. "We're all in history, that's sure, but some are more than others, Jews more than some."[16] This feeling of being snowed under by history is not simply the consequence of Bok's departure from the shtetl. His parents had remained in the shtetl and "the historical evil had galloped in to murder them there."[17] Bok concludes, "In or out, it was history that counted—the world's bad memory. It remembered the wrong things."[18] But rather than be overcome by it and rather than flee it, Bok wills to stand against it. As he says in his dream to Bibikov, "Something in myself has

15. Ibid., p. 305.
16. Ibid., p. 314.
17. Ibid., p. 315.
18. Ibid.

changed. I'm not the same man I was. I fear less and hate more."[19]
His hatred and resistance almost spoil Bok's goal of a trial, as he
strikes out at the deputy warden when insulted, and he is saved
when a guard interferes and is shot in Bok's stead.

As he rides to his trial, Bok creates in his mind a scene in which
his program of Jewish hatred and resistance is projected on a grand
scale. He imagines an interview with the Tsar in which Bok accuses
him of causing the bad conditions of Russia for both Jews and
impoverished Gentiles. In retaliation he shoots the Tsar, saying
"This is also for the prison, the poison, the six daily searches. It's
for Bibikov and Kogin [the guard shot in his stead] and for a lot
more that I won't even mention."[20] Bok has moved from being a
non-Jew, to being a passive suffering Jew, and finally to becoming
a militant Jew, an agent in history active against evil on behalf of
his own integrity and his suffering people. To that end, Bok vows
to abolish his nonpolitical attitude. To be a Jew means also to be
a political man, for "where there's no fight for it there's no freedom." "Death to the anti-Semites! Long live revolution! Long live
liberty!"[21]

The Fixer arises out of interests which, as we shall see, form a
common core in Malamud's body of fiction. For one thing, the
pattern of dying and rising is present, as it is in his other full-length
works. Bok comes out of the living death of his cell with new
direction and determination. In addition, the protagonist is, as are
Malamud's other principal characters, a disillusioned pilgrim. He
moves toward Kiev in the hope of a new life, and he pursues
money as a life-giving resource. But what he encounters in Kiev
and in the circles of wealth is not life but death: racial antipathy,
the call to deny his own integrity, name, and origins, and moral
decay. With the arrest, pilgrimage is exchanged for stasis. Then the
true, valid journey begins, the internal one, Bok's move to personal
resources from which the shape and significance for his new life are
drawn. Finally, as in the other books, surrounding darkness is
present in this book. Like the protagonist of *The Natural*, Bok is

19. Ibid., p. 319.
20. Ibid., p. 334.
21. Ibid., p. 335.

gripped by powers which he cannot control, powers which he can, at the end, only defy. Like the judge in *The Natural*, the Tsar is aloof, manipulating Bok's fate in his hiddenness. In addition, Bok is tossed around on a dark sea of superstitions, anti-Semitism, and blood accusation. He is dwarfed by this darkness, this unpredictable and irrational threat. While a pilgrim he underestimated this darkness, but in the cell, during the investigation, and in the indictment he learns its profundity well. When he faces his situation, Bok discovers for the first time the content of "I," of his own identity and integrity. He no longer looks to riches beyond himself which will fulfill him; he no longer spends himself in self-canceling pursuits. Instead, he mines the rich resources of his internal life and comes to a decision which clarifies his identity, the decision not to escape his history.

Despite the similarity to his other works, there appears in this one something new: a strident militancy, a kind of Jewish-power. Bok's intention at the end is to answer suffering by inflicting it, to turn from victim to assailant. This spirit arises out of a hope that the enemy can be localized, in this case localized in the person of the Tsar, and that a better, more life-producing political structure can be formed. To use the terms of Albert Camus, Bok has turned at the end from a rebel into a revolutionary, from saying "no" against the powers which attempt to intimidate and bribe him to saying "yes" to a new political and social order that lies as a possibility beyond the present one. Bok at the end is journeying again, moving from stasis to revolution. He moves from the courage of charity to the courage of the kill.

The revolutionary emphasis at the end is a bit abrupt because throughout the work pilgrimage, movement both in time and in space, is revealed to be a self-falsifying act, a clutching at impure paradises. In his revolutionary attitude, Bok is moving again, this time toward a new social order. In addition, the enemy, anti-Semitism, has been revealed throughout the work as too general and too deep in the subrational life of the people to be localized in any one person. But at the end Bok identifies this otherwise impersonal, indefinite enemy as the Tsar.

The process by which Bok is stripped of all hope is the most memorable moment in the work. Bok recognizes that history, which he had been taught to believe was touched by God's presence, is without meaning and antagonistic to Jewish identity and life. With this recognition, Bok resolves to resist demonic, anti-Semitic history to the end, to affirm his identity, integrity, and relation to his people regardless of the pressures against him. The process of disillusionment, then, the experience of God's absence, leads to the actualization of Bok's selfhood, of what it means to be a Jew and a man.

II

As I pointed out in the Introduction and in my opening comments on *The Fixer*, a person need not be a member of the "death of God" school of theology to locate moments in contemporary life in which the word "God" seems to be inappropriate or in which it seems to lack meaning. One moment occurs in that side of life which we have freed from religious norms and language, the world of public institutions and activity. Although it is possible to over-evaluate this public world so that its nonreligious character is thought to suggest the nonreligious character of *all* of life, there is also no way of denying that this world is a major component of our experience and tends to overshadow what is not included in it. A second moment occurs in relation to objects or events which are the products of human intentions. When we can quite adequately account for the existence or meaning of things and events without the language of religion, bringing it in seems a gratuitous, even meaningless, act. Finally, the word "God" seems inappropriate or meaningless in relation to an object or event that deeply contradicts what we desire or intend. Although a religious man would affirm that God is unlike anything else in our world, and although an event such as gratuitous suffering can become, as it does for Job, a spiritual discipline, an object or event which directly contradicts what we know or desire destroys the ability to see the word "God" as deriving its meaning from what we experience; it must be taken as a word which derives its force and meaning from something outside of our world. Even if it gains meaning in this way, the point remains that the word "God" is not meaningful in direct association with such an object or event.

The consequence of the loss of appropriateness or meaning for the word "God" is that the sense of an ordering, inclusive center is lost. Without a will and intention behind his world, a man feels that he and his fellows are left as vulnerable, precious instances of awareness in an otherwise mindless, accidental universe. This feeling is a particularly troubling one when the absence of God is felt in or because of an experience of gratuitous suffering or loss. The victim of the suffering, assaulted by the immediate event, finds no comfort behind or beyond it.

In Bernard Malamud's fiction the characters are often in deep need of a world ordered and enriched by reference to transcendent will and design. They are often people on a journey looking for what they do not have, an ordering or life-giving center. They are often on a quest or a pilgrimage. In each case, whether they are pilgrims, such as Bok, who think they know where the life-giving center is, or questers uncertain of its location, or uncertain that it can be found, the results are similar. They conclude that there is no ordering or life-giving center. The holy is gone, and they conclude their journeys by standing still, by affirming what remains despite that loss or by holding their own during the absence of sacredness.

Quest is quite central to *The Natural*[22] (1952), and most readers of it have recognized its dependence upon *La Queste de Saint Graal*. Roy Hobbs plays baseball for the Knights; he uses a lance-bat; he is managed by Pop Fisher; and he brings rain. In addition, Roy's appetites remind us of Jessie Weston's view that the Grail legend may have its origin in sexual rituals.[23]

Roy's quest fails for several reasons. He gets little help from his guides or surrogate fathers, for Sam Simpson and Pop Fisher have never achieved their own goals and never will. In addition, Roy underestimates the forces of darkness and destruction around him.

22. Bernard Malamud, *The Natural* (New York: Farrar, Straus and Giroux, 1952).

23. Jessie L. Weston, *From Ritual to Romance* (Cambridge: Cambridge University Press, 1920).

He misunderstands the intentions of Harriet Bird, who plots his execution, and of Memo, the agent of the manipulating judge who stands above Roy in the dark tower, and of the gambler Gus, who inhabits the world below in the dark Pot of Fire. The third reason is Roy's selfishness. He seems to want what he thinks is best for him, Memo and baseball glory, and he becomes frantic when his increasing age makes the two more and more unattainable. At the end he lunges for one of his goals, Memo, and rejects the other by throwing the play-off game.

Roy has two alternatives granted him after the failure of the quest, defiance and Iris Lemon. He chooses defiance, and, although this gives his life some integrity, it seems to be not as fortunate as the alternative Iris offers: to live in the present without nostalgia for the past or longing for the future. Her life-giving attitude is one of waiting, and, at the end, when everything has been lost, Roy has peace in waiting with Iris for the birth of their son.

Wandering is the significant form of journey in *The Assistant*[24] (1957), and it follows a pattern similar to *The Natural*. Frank Alpine changes from a man on the move to a man who stays. Both violent and gentle by nature, an anti-Semite and an admirer of St. Francis, Frank first steals from and then returns to work for Morris Bober. For a short time he is content to work in the store, but he soon begins to cheat Morris and to peek at the Bobers' daughter, Helen. Morris takes him in because of his own fatigue. A disillusioned pilgrim-immigrant, Morris has gotten little from life in America. And his daughter is getting little more. Drawn by the ideal of an educated and refined life, she is discontent with what her situation and the men she knows can offer her. The three get on rather well, initially. Frank gives gifts to Helen; he becomes more appreciative of Jews; and business picks up. But the three are also uneasy. Morris suspects Frank of stealing; Helen holds herself back because Frank is not Jewish and because her chief interest is in education; and Frank is impatient with marginal living. When Frank is caught stealing and when he rapes Helen the relationships are broken.

24. Bernard Malamud, *The Assistant* (New York: Farrar, Straus and Giroux, 1957).

THE DEATH OF GOD

The third part of the plot, including chapters six through nine, is very dark. Frank loathes himself, Helen is disillusioned, and Morris gets no help in his impoverished condition either from Jews or from employment agencies. Pathetically, Morris, in an unusually free and ecstatic mood, shovels snow and overly taxes his decayed health. In the midst of these unfortunate events, Frank decides to take Morris's place in the store.

In the final chapter, which is different from the others in pace and tone, things improve: the business, Frank's relation to Helen, and his self-esteem. At the end Frank seals his decision and new life with circumcision and, after Passover, becomes a Jew.

This work has several levels. At the societal level it depicts the life of an identifiable ethnic and economic group. At the psychic level it uncovers a pursuit of suffering which, though somewhat masochistic, serves to actualize the self. At the mythic level it depicts the death and rising of Frank who dies as a lost boy and rises as a worthy son. At the level of its religious ideas it clarifies what being a Jew means. Although Frank encounters many under-standings of what it means to be a Jew, he forms his own by uniting the Judaism of Morris, the ability to suffer, the strength to stay, and the sense of family, to an asceticism Frank has learned from St. Francis. Frank embraces poverty and loneliness as Morris could not. The alternative to the journey or wandering is a spiritual blend which allows Frank to live despite the loss of God's presence.

Although standing in one place may be more suitable to the short story form than journeying, the characters in the stories of *The Magic Barrel*[25] (1958) are often on the move, and their journeys lead to disillusionment. For example, Mitka in "The Girl of My Dreams" is disillusioned when the girl he finally meets is a victim of more suffering then Mitka can handle. Similarly, Leo Finkle is drawn by his quest for a wife into the troubling world of poverty and cruelty. The pilgrims are not more fortunate. Carl Schneider in "Behold the Key" is a disillusioned pilgrim to Rome, the land of his dreams, for he finds there confusion, bribery, and inhospitality. Henry Levin is equally unsuccessful on his pilgrimage

25. Bernard Malamud, *The Magic Barrel* (New York: Farrar, Straus and Cudahy, 1958).

THE FIXER

in "The Lady of the Lake." Trying to overcome a sense of inferiority, he denies his religion, identity, and name in the process of traveling first to Europe and then to the exotic Isola del Dongo, the home of the aristocratic Isabella del Dongo. When the girl turns out to be a poor Jewish refugee, Henry, having lost himself in the pilgrimage, loses the girl, too. And Arthur Fidelman is a pilgrim, heading toward the historic and aesthetic riches of Rome. But the real pilgrimage he undergoes is to the synagogue, cemetery, and ghetto of Rome where he confronts suffering, oppression, and death.

As common as these instances of journey are examples of standing still. The opening story, "The First Seven Years," renders the great strength necessary for standing. And Kessler in "The Mourners" is such a sticker that his landlord cannot evict him. Kessler's tenacity grants wisdom both to himself and to the landlord, and at the end the two sit together in mourning.

Of course there are distortions possible in standing still, such as those suggested by the escapist character of the isolated lives of the young men in "The Magic Barrel" and "The Girl of My Dreams." Similarly, Manischevitz has achieved an elevated sense of his spiritual importance, and the Negro Jew, Angel Levine, must reveal to him the suffering of other people, especially Negroes, so that Manischevitz will see that there are Jews everywhere. "Take Pity" presents a woman who rejects the help of other people out of pride, revealing the results of unnecessary isolation and deprivation. (A similar distortion can be seen in "The Bill.") Standing still can also be a form of deception, as it is in "A Summer's Reading"; the boy in this story, although idle, falsely creates the self-image of an active reader. Finally, isolation can become self-imprisonment, as it does for Tommy Castelli in "The Prison" and for the baker's wife in "The Loan." But despite the distortions and unfortunate consequences that may arise from the life of standing, standing is a more creative, life-giving exercise than wandering, quest, or pilgrimage.

The pilgrim of *A New Life*[26] (1961), S. Levin, learns that newness of life is not granted by some special place or by a new career

26. Bernard Malamud, *A New Life* (New York: Farrar, Straus and Cudahy, 1961).

but by possibilities which lie more immediately at hand. Leaving behind his old, hopeless existence in New York for the promises of the West Coast and college teaching, Levin quickly discovers that he is an outsider in Cascadia. The victim of very funny situations, the only single man in a married community, an ex-drunk amidst temperance leaders, a political liberal among reactionaries, and an idealist among pragmatists, his pilgrimage brings only disillusionment. The people associated with his new job make him very uneasy, especially his paternalistic and authoritarian departmental chairman and his colleague Gerald Gilley. In the second part of the book, the second quarter of the school year, Levin's feeling of disillusionment grows, and it is balanced by his love affair with his colleague's wife, Pauline. Although this affair becomes the life-giving center in an otherwise disappointing world, Levin feels he must end the affair because of the awkward and unnerving existence it creates. Levin decides, instead, to give life to his world by fighting what he dislikes in his department. In the final developments of the plot he carries on his crusade for freedom, human values, and the liberal arts. But his efforts are frustrated. Levin turns from his fight back to Pauline, and the two go off at the end as exiles from a paradise that never was.

Levin's disillusionment as a pilgrim testifies to the absence of grace, for Levin finds no life-giving center. His ability to accept Pauline's love was an ability always within him; it is no different from his ability to see in a New York cellar the value resident in a chair when the sun strikes it. Such moments constitute the holy in life. They are isolated, largely internal, and not the effects of pilgrimage or quest.

A character very similar to S. Levin is Cronin in "A Choice of Profession," one of the stories from *Idiots First*[27] (1963). But unlike Levin, Cronin cannot embrace the present, and he is unworthy of his girl friend's honesty and trust. In "Still Life," Arthur Fidelman is not a pilgrim but a quester who seeks the treasures of Rome, aesthetic life, and sexual fulfillment. But the treasures constantly elude his grasp. When he finally grasps still life, when he

27. Bernard Malamud, *Idiots First* (New York: Farrar, Straus and Co., 1963).

paints what he sees in his friend and in himself, intimacy and fulfillment result. Fidelman also appears in "Naked Nude," an unusually cheerful piece in the Malamud corpus.

Several of these stories are very bleak. In "The Cost of Living"
we are given a grocer who, like Morris Bober, is destroyed by
forces he cannot resist. And in "The German Refugee" Malamud
gives us an exile from Nazi Germany who finds that the destruction
of his former home and his wife by the Nazis is too much for him
to bear. These characters do not experience the kind of assistance
in the crises of life that comes to Mendel in the title story. His good
fortune is in Malamud's world a rare instance of grace received
from without.

If we can generalize on these stories, on the continuation of
Fidelman's zany, poignant quest in *Pictures of Fidelman*,[28] and on
all of Malamud's fiction, it is fair to say that, in his juxtaposition of
journey and stasis, journey is generally found to be a disillusioning
and ineffective tack. It is so because there are no life-giving, ordering centers which a man can find or toward which he can move.
More promising is standing, grasping the present, being true to
what is within, and making the most of possibilities which lie at
hand. The modest optimism which emerges from his work depends
on the austerity and integrity which can be secured by faithful
endurance in the face of the absence of grace.

III

In the year of Samuel's *Blood Accusation* and Malamud's *The
Fixer*, Rabbi Richard Rubenstein published a collection of essays
entitled *After Auschwitz: Radical Theology and Contemporary
Judaism*.[29] It has affinities with the other two books because it
takes up the challenge to Jewish life and thought created by the
horrors of anti-Semitism in this century. In addition, it expresses
the same dissatisfaction with traditional Jewish covenant theology

28. Bernard Malamud, *Pictures of Fidelman: An Exhibition* (New York:
Farrar, Straus and Giroux, 1969).
29. Richard L. Rubenstein, *After Auschwitz: Radical Theology and Contemporary Judaism* (Indianapolis: Bobbs-Merrill Co., Inc., 1966).

which Yakov Bok feels especially in the second part of *The Fixer*'s plot.

The history of Jews has been determined, since the rise of the Christian church, by Christianity. Jews have moved, suffered, flourished, or been repressed by Christian whim and caprice. The lord of Jewish history has been Christianity, and Christianity, often representing a deadly power and never being fully trustworthy for the Jew, can easily be seen by the Jew as an expression of evil. Since their history has been dominated by non-Jews or at times by anti-Jews, it is possible that Jews will consider history as evil.

Rabbi Rubenstein points to the murder of six million Jews by the Nazis as an event which confirms, if it had not been confirmed before, that anti-Semites, people evil for Jews, have been the lords of Jewish history and not God. Covenant theology is dead; history is evil; one can even say that God is dead.

Rabbi Rubenstein feels that upon recognizing the evil of history, the Jew must neither ignore that evil nor deny his own Jewishness. The Jew must embrace and affirm his nature and destiny.

> We did not ask to be born; we did not ask for our absurd existence in the world; nor have we asked for the fated destiny which has hung about us as Jews. Yet we would not exchange it, nor would we deny it, for when nothing is asked for, nothing is hoped for, nothing is expected; all that we receive is truly grace.[30]

Rubenstein believes that there is no final answer in history itself to its evils, to the tragic separation between men, the disappointing character of human experience and relationships, and the deep internal tensions which plague a man. The only resolution to these problems, which are more the consequences or marks of existence in general than of peculiarly Jewish history, is death. There is no solution in history; to be in history is to be in evil. To be out of history, if there is a solution out of history, is to be dead.

Short of death, the only creative response to the evil history is the cultivation of sacred place. Rubenstein moves from the historical-prophetic to the spatial-priestly in his move from God to religion.

30. Ibid., pp. 128–29.

The European catastrophe marks the death of the God of History; the re-establishment of Israel marks the rebirth of the long-forgotten Gods of Earth within Jewish experience.[31]

In a religion of history, history as a linear movement from a beginning to an end, man and God are the lively components; nature is relatively unimportant, even dead. As Rubenstein sees the divine-human history as dead, overcome by the demonic, especially anti-Semitism, he sees the natural world take on life. A religion of the earth is not a way of talking about God but a way of giving order to our lives and unity to our community. If we can speak of God at all it is in a mystical fashion: God is Nothingness into which a man is drawn at death.[32]

Although Rubenstein equates death with God and the Messiah, he feels that death ought not to be sought. Of greater value is human and natural life which must be purified to goodness and beauty by a deep dedication to the discipline of law. Law for him, as for the whole tradition, is life-enhancing and not life-denying. It provides the possibility of life and an alternative to unstructured, victimizing chaos. Rubenstein believes that, in a time such as the present, structure, order, and tradition are needed more than ever before.[33]

Rabbi Rubenstein has illuminated a painful but inescapable problem in religious life and thought: the loss of meaning in the word "God" when that word is used in relation to what a man feels contradicts his own sense of what is just or true. It is a painful problem because it is at moments of catastrophe that one most deeply needs the power of God's name, and it is painful because the loss of meaning at some moment implies the meaninglessness of all moments.

It may be helpful to see that the Bible is not without instances of gratuitous suffering and the sense of meaninglessness. First we should see the many ways in which suffering is given meaning in the Bible before looking at moments of the absence of meaning.

31. Ibid., p. 130.
32. Ibid., p. 136.
33. Richard Rubenstein, "Judaism and the Death of God," *Playboy* 14, no. 7 (July 1967), p. 74.

The first way in which meaning is given to suffering is in terms of the past. Pain is not arbitrary; it can be seen in relationship to aspects of history. Most immediately this is a reference to the individual's or community's sins. The most striking illustration of this is the Deuteronomic historian who interprets the people's subjection by a hostile nation as the immediate consequence of their infidelity. Also from an orientation to things past comes the answer that we suffer for the sins of our parents. There is a kind of fatalism in this view, namely, that suffering is unavoidable. The sins of previous generations have their effects on us now, and there is little we can do about it. The attitude rests on a firm understanding of the centrality of the community. As the individual is given his life by the community, so the community of the present is given its life by the community of the past. The dark corollary of this view is the transference into the present of not only the life but also the consequences of evil in former generations, evil that comes down to "the third and fourth generation." So common a notion was this at the time of the destruction of Jerusalem that Jeremiah and Ezekiel had to speak directly to the idea and challenge it because the people became resigned to evil and did not repent, since they tended to minimize the significance of the present in comparison to the load of effects deposited on them by the past. A kind of Karma, this working out on one generation the effects of the lives of previous generations, seems to have gripped the people at some points in their history. Finally, the past provides meaning to suffering because in the beginning man introduced evil into the world. This is a more ultimate understanding because it represents an attempt by the people to understand their own time of suffering in the middle of time by seeing their present in relation to an ultimate beginning and end. Beginning and end are without suffering and evil. There is a sense of fallenness, of being down here in this time of evil and suffering. We are in this mess because we are not any longer at the beginning; we have a name and a place because Yahweh is bringing us and the earth to a new end, his holiness.

The future also provides some resources for meaning in evil and suffering. The first instance is the awareness of suffering as a part of a process. It is essential to the process of creation because in the process something is destroyed so that the new creation can be formed. Redemptive events in the Bible follow the pattern of creation stories more closely than does the creation hymn of Genesis 1, which is a theological, priestly lyric. Essential to a creation story is struggle and the domination of resisting, evil forces. The two great creation stories in the Bible are the Exodus and the conquest of Canaan. Suffering is a part of these stories because the people are caught in a grand, cosmic drama and get hurt, although those on the wrong side are much worse off. This pattern of conflict-creation is also discernible in the prophet's messages. More and more a critical period is described by them, a moment of breaking down and building up, a moment of destruction and re-creation. Another way in which suffering is given meaning by the future is revealed in Second Isaiah. The suffering servant passages refer to an expiation by suffering. A victim, probably the community, suffers in order to bear away the hostility and evil of others. Meaning is given to suffering not in terms of cause but in terms of effect, not from forces in the past but of results in the future. As we view this communal or individual sufferer we believe that our sins and our pain are taken away by his suffering, that by him we are healed. How this process takes place is hard to say, as hard to determine as the identity of this sufferer. This way of seeing meaning in suffering is relatively minor in the Bible, although it becomes more important in Judaism and becomes all-important for Christianity.

These are the more proximate, immediate interpretations of suffering in the Bible. In all of them God is not gone; he is allowing something to happen or he is doing something which results in pain but which is necessary and meaningful. I want now to indicate more ultimate understandings of evil. The first is that evil is chaos. When a new creation arises out of God's struggle with evil, the new creation is surrounded by chaos. The people's world is surrounded by chaos, water, which God actively holds back. When the people do evil they fall back into chaos or they allow chaos to enter the order and overcome it. Evil is chaos, evidence that the people, or the land, and the law have not yet called into being the end. Evil is the opposite of God's presence and work; it is confusion, disorder, and meaninglessness.

In this understanding, evil stands apart from God, but evil is too mysterious an element or power to be so isolated. Evil is also associated with God. God is not only creative; he is also destructive. His presence melts the rocks. Those who touch his holiness or who happen to be in the way when he passes by get hurt. God's presence is antithetical to man's presence. People must stay out of his way, and they may not presume on him; he does what he pleases and no one is to call him into account.

In both cases evil is mysterious. It is not part of a scheme, deriving its place from something that transcends it. Evil, with the pain it brings, is itself transcendent, at one time God's opposite, at another the consequence of his approach.

In these ways, then, suffering is made meaningful in the Bible, but there are also moments of suffering and evil in which God is not present. I would like to draw attention to two of these, one personal and the other communal, times when God is gone and suffering is arbitrary, gratuitous, and meaningless.

The most important, because it is part of the community's memory, is the slavery in Egypt. Speaking of Egypt this way is difficult for two reasons, one historical and the other literary. Some scholars doubt the historicity of the Egypt-Exodus experiences; they doubt the history of Israel prior to the settling of Canaan. Indeed, the memory of these things is different from Israel's memories associated with the land. Secondly, it is doubtful that the memory of Egypt included very much, if any, agony over what went on during the dark years of slavery. Very little is said in the Bible about this period of darkness. Where was God between the death of Joseph and the call of Moses? For a while things go well for the people, but then they are victimized by a political and historical fact. A new Pharaoh arises who knows nothing of Joseph. The results are dreadful; God is gone. I want to return to this, perhaps imaginative, Egypt later. First, let us look at the moment of individual awareness of God's departure and consequent meaningless suffering.

There are two instances of individual meaningless suffering, Ecclesiastes and Job. Pointless suffering must have bothered the great poet who took the original story of Job and added the long, poetic section in which Job struggles in darkness with his friends and, more importantly, with God. In one sense this poetic section is a great attack on attempts to see meaning in suffering. Job does not suffer because of sins. There is no scheme or process of which Job's experiences can be seen as a part. And God's presence is not to be seen in suffering. Evil is arbitrary and inexplicable. Job's suffering, however terrible and gratuitous, is meaningful because it forms a kind of discipline by which Job is prepared for his mystical apprehension and communion with God at the end. The mystery of evil is maintained, but the experience is not all loss; it is a fire in which Job is softened for his new relationship with God. Ecclesiastes is a more difficult matter. Qoheleth moves in a world without meaning. The dominating element in his world is death which cancels out all meaning. Life moves without apparent reason toward no apparent goal. But again, suffering, especially the pain of disillusionment and awareness of death, is a discipline which leads to insight (Eccles. 9:7–10 and 11:7–10). The discipline of disillusionment is rigorous and humiliating, but it leads to wisdom and honesty. Suffering is a stern but effective teacher.

No meaning or use can be seen, however, in the darkness and pain of Egypt, and Egypt remains the great black hole of the Bible, unexplained, unapproachable. Egypt is a great unanswered question in the Bible, and the hasty narration rushes over the pit. Where was God while the people suffered in Egypt? The only answer is that the suffering was arbitrary and pointless, and God was gone. It is with the people's back to this pit that the whole Bible is written, and the pit is never entered again, not even during the Exile[34] and the Diaspora, until the Second World War.

The religious man cannot give meaning to the pit of gratuitous suffering. He can only talk fast as he passes over it, can only turn his back on it and speak loudly in the other direction. Martin Buber expresses this inability beautifully in his address of 1953 to the

---

34. However, the Exile is at some moments understood to be a moment of God's departure:
> In overflowing wrath for a moment
> I hid my face from you,
> but with everlasting love I will have
> compassion on you,
> says the Lord, your Redeemer (Isa. 54:8).

German people. The address was given on the occasion of the award to Buber of the Peace Prize of the German Book Trade at Frankfurt, and it is entitled "Genuine Dialogue and the Possibilities of Peace." After expressing his thanks for the award Buber says to these Germans:

> About a decade ago a considerable number of Germans—there must have been many thousands of them—under the indirect command of the German government and the direct command of its representatives, killed millions of my people in a systematically prepared and executed procedure whose organized cruelty cannot be compared with any previous historical event. I, who am one of those who remained alive, have only in a formal sense a common humanity with those who took part in this action. They have so radically removed themselves from the human sphere, so transposed themselves into a sphere of monstrous inhumanity inaccessible to my conception, that not even hatred, much less an overcoming of hatred, was able to arise in me. And what am I that I could here presume to 'forgive'![35]

The event "cannot be compared with any previous historical event," one cannot comprehend it, and those who were responsible lie outside of "the human sphere." With faithful religious intuition, Buber says nothing about the event and about those responsible. He turns his back on them, speaking away from *homo contrahumanus* and towards *homo humanus*.

An experience of the absence of God is, for the religious man, the experience of arbitrary and meaningless suffering, the experience of horror; otherwise, the absence of God from human life is a consequence of man's forgetting or ignoring God, of having no place for, or sensing no need of, God. Buber's contribution to "death of God" reflection is not as much his *Eclipse of God* as his address to the German people. The experience of gratuitous suffering, of meaningless pain, corresponds with the experience that God is gone.

Evil of the magnitude of the holocaust is not a problem which creates or refutes theological categories. Such an evil, gratuitous,

---

35. Martin Buber, *Pointing the Way,* trans. and ed. Maurice Friedman (London: Routledge and Kegan Paul, 1957), p. 232. Reprinted with permission of Harper & Row, Inc.

meaningless suffering and the absence of God, is not reducible to the status of problem. It is a mystery before which one can stand in awe and dread.

The sense of God's absence and the sense of God's presence point to the deepest of religious experiences, but, as so often happens at such moments, the language in which they are expressed, perhaps because the language must always be inadequate to the experience, becomes superficially used. On the one hand, people speak or sing of being on friendly terms with God, being held in his hand; just as superficially people speak of the death of God, as though remarking something not much different from the fact that the Edsel car is no longer manufactured. People who speak lightly about the death of God are no more profound or religiously interesting than those who speak lightly of, as it is put in *Zooey*, spending four minutes every day with the Almighty.

I think that we face the danger today of producing and reading fictions which take the matter of God's absence as lightly and in as unearned a way as novels, which are still being published by denominational presses, once ended with Jane's naughty boyfriend finally meeting God. The situation is paralleled in theology where "God is dead" is no more profound than "Jesus saves."

The death of God can no more be an established cultural fact than can be the presence of God. People will continue to claim one or the other experience, but both must always be experienced anew. Perhaps a reverse kind of prophetic work needs to be done by thoughtful people in our time. While the prophets had to attack their contemporaries for taking God's presence for granted, perhaps taking God's absence as a given fact, unearned and unexperienced, should be challenged today. Too much that passes as the sense of God's absence is no less superficial and secondhand than the feeling that God loves me and all other Lutherans (in our Synod!).

The danger, in short, is in the loss of feeling and depth, a danger that threatens both the theological and the literary worlds. The spectacle of talents in both areas competing with one another, this one on one tack, that one on another, seems truer of the religious and literary situations than the presence of visionaries. In this situation readers cannot become equally superficial, diminishing their criteria. Fortunately, we continue to be blessed with writers and religious thinkers who refresh us or deepen our awareness. There are times when the writers and theologians discussed in this study have been able to do this. And there are many more. But in a time when fiction is big business and when theologians seem talked out, we ought to be wary of vision that is only masked flippancy; the present emphasis in literature and theology on the death of God or the experience of meaningless can easily become, if it is not already, just that.

5

The Confessions of Nat Turner
and the Dynamic of Revolution

The preoccupations which we found characterizing the other fiction treated in this study are also present in Styron's Pulitzer Prize-winning novel, *The Confessions of Nat Turner*. The inadequacy of clergy is exposed again, in this case by three men who speak both from great personal weaknesses and in eager support of slavery. Dr. Ballard, the least repulsive of the three, rejects Samuel Turner's humanitarian attitudes toward the slaves in favor of the position that Negroes are little more than animals with children's brains. Richard Whitehead, the local Methodist pastor, speaks, in a "high-pitched and effeminate"[1] voice, words formulated by the bishop of Virginia and calculated "to make the Negroes stand in mortal fear."[2] Finally, the Reverend Alexander Eppes, a sadistic homosexual, hardly deserves Samuel Turner's confidence in him, a confidence caused by a "traditional respect for and trust in the goodness of the clergy" and judged by Nat Turner to be "a central mistake."[3] Whatever faults Styron attributes to the whites of Virginia, the clergy possess them in a concentrated form.

Transcendent power is also felt in the work through Nat Turner's consciousness. It is a power expressed most immediately through the domination of black history and identity by white antipathy and

1. William Styron, *The Confessions of Nat Turner* (New York: Random House, 1967), p. 96.
2. Ibid., p. 97.
3. Ibid., p. 239.

evil. Gradually, however, transcendent power also becomes a source and impetus for Nat's attack on the power of oppression. Transcendent power is primarily antagonistic, however, and Nat is even uncertain, after the revolution, whether transcendent power did provide a resource and justification for his actions.

Nat's feelings of the absence of God, his loneliness at the end, continue the general sense of meaninglessness which we found in *The Blood of the Lamb* and, especially, in *The Fixer*. Nat's inability to see the presence of God in any objective structure or event leaves him, at the end, with grave doubts about divine favor and the success or meaning of his revolution.

Finally, the matter of vocation is obviously central to this work. It should be mentioned that all feel it, the whites as well as the blacks, for the general sense of malaise or degeneration which several of the whites express adds to the atmosphere of crisis. The times do not provide men with meaningful work; tobacco is repeatedly mentioned as a product unworthy of Virginia's natural and human resources. This sense of crisis, this tension between internal desires or needs and external activity, is sharply focused in the terribly dehumanizing position of the slave.

Added to preoccupations we have encountered in the other works is the call to social revolution, a call issued primarily at the end of *The Fixer* but central to this work. The emphasis is somewhat strange in American fiction, and it has very little place in the literature of the authors here studied. True, Don Wanderhope shakes his fist at the sky, but the general character of the work of these authors is quietistic. Revolutionary attitudes and their sociological, psychological, and ontological bases are not as central to American writers as they are to Europeans such as Silone, Kazantzakis, and Camus.

The question of rebellion and social violence brings up the matter of the black revolution, its literature, and the relation of Styron's work to it. On occasion *The Confessions of Nat Turner* has suffered public burning at meetings of black students, the contention being that this book is another exploitation by whites of black resources, a white intrusion into black psychology and a white interpretation of black revolution. Postponing comment on that relationship until later, it should be stated here that Styron's interest in Nat Turner is not primarily historical or racial. As Malamud used the Beiliss affair, Styron has taken this event to render fictionally themes which appear in his other works as well, primarily the occasion, sources, and goals of revolution. Although the material which Styron used is an actual revolution led by a black slave, his principal interest seems to lie in the resource of confessional fiction and in the phenomenon of a revolutionary act.

I

Although he is not black, while Malamud is Jewish, Styron has used black experience in this work as Malamud tends to use Jewish life: as a way of bringing into sharp focus what people generally experience sporadically. As he says in his apologetic note, the work is not a historical novel but a meditation on history. It is, I would say, an imaginative rendering of the revolutionary consciousness, and the historical situation is used to epitomize those aspects of attitude and circumstance which are true of a revolutionary mentality or event.

Tone, subjective presence, is the principal fictional element in this work. What is arresting about the stance and attitude of the narrator is that he appears, in his confession, to be working through questions, reliving events, and gaining insight while he narrates. The effect of the narrating, then, is not, as Nat tells Mr. Gray, to give public expression to his cause, what may be the effect of the confession read in court, but to clarify problems with which Nat is wrestling and to reach personal solutions to them. This principal effect of Nat's narrating is tied to his dealings with Gray by the fact that some of Gray's questions stimulate Nat's struggle, especially questions about the number of blacks who supported the revolution and about Nat's timidity in killing. Perhaps it is also stimulated by Gray's ridicule of Christian faith and by his insistence in court on Nat's inherent inferiority, since religion is so central to Nat's struggle and since he is so eager to stress, especially through Margaret Whitehead's estimation of him, his own spiritual and intellectual gifts. Primarily, however, the confession seems stimulated by the agonizing possibility that, because the revolution was as much a disappointment to Nat as an actualization of his expectations, it lacked justification and meaningfulness. Simultaneous with the account of the rebellion stands Nat's experiences after the revolution of rejection by God, loneliness, and God's forgiveness and acceptance in and through the person of Margaret Whitehead.

In the process of working through his actions and thoughts, Nat gives us the occasion, sources, and goals of revolution. The occasion rests in the general declining situation, in the evils of the time, economic, social, and moral, and in those forces ruining Virginia, tobacco and slavery. The sources of revolution are personal and racial pride, psychic and physical energy, and transcendent, divine approbation. The goals of the revolution are revenge, catharsis, and the reconciliation of estranged goods.

The theme of decline and degeneration is voiced at many points in the narrative. The decline of Virginia and the evil of the times reaffirm the statement quoted from Nat's stolen Bunyan: "It is folly to look for good days so long as sin is so high, and those that study its nourishment so many. . . ."[4] Judge Cobb and Samuel Turner express a deep dismay over what Virginia has become, exploited and despoiled by greed for money and the cultivation of tobacco. Cobb calls Virginia "a cornucopia of riches the like of which the world has never seen, transformed within the space of a century to a withering, defeated hag!"[5] Turner sees a bleak end as inevitable:

> "Well, soon all of them will be gone—everything—not just the land now utterly consumed by that terrible weed, not just the wagons and the pigs and the oxen and the mules but the men too, the white men and the women and the black boys—the Willies and the Jims and the Shadrachs and the Todds—all gone south, leaving Virginia to the thorn bushes and the dandelions."[6]

These judgments are confirmed by Nat's picture of this society. It is a society of white gentility that masks vicious and decadent racial and sexual attitudes, a contrast the slaves can see as they observe

4. Ibid., p. 138.
5. Ibid., p. 68.
6. Ibid., p. 220.

unnoticed the private lives of their masters. As Nat suggests several times, the revolutionary mind can be developed only in blacks who know the whites, know their hypocrisy, fears, and immoralities.

This white duplicity is matched by a duplicity the whites force on the blacks, their docility and agreeableness concealing a smouldering resentment and hate. Consequently, the whites, except for Cobb and Turner, live in the illusion of harmony and peace, ignorant of the private feelings of blacks while exposing to the blacks white weaknesses and sin.

The state of degeneration is so complete that no toehold in the situation can be secured for the amelioration of evils. Hope in the future is, then, at best an illusion, and, more often, it is an unfortunate escape from the horrible realities of the present. Samuel Turner is most guilty of this illusion and escape. While expressing a vision of the decay of the present, he has enough confidence in some other people that he charts a plan for Nat's training and emancipation which is supported by fancy and crushed by realities. With a loss of confidence in the future, Nat turns to the resources of the present.

The first of the resources Nat taps for his revolutionary act is individual and group pride. Although Nat Turner knows nothing about his father except that he had run away after being struck in the face by his master, what he knows is formative. Nat's mother says, "Said he couldn' stand to be hit in de face by nobody. Not *nobody!* Oh yes, dat black man had pride, awright, warn't many black mens aroun' like him!"[7] A sense of personal pride, Nat feels, is an indispensable source for the revolution. Without it the conviction that a value has been violated by slavery cannot be fostered. However, personal pride is a rare attribute among Styron's slaves, and Nat miscalculates the number who would rise with him against the injustice of their situation. For this reason the fact is several times mentioned that indispensable for revolution is a lenient or humanitarian owner, for, by removing the pressure on the slave or by treating him as a person, the owner gives the slave the room or the impetus to think of himself as valuable. When that sense develops, the slave comes to realize the horror of his position.

7. Ibid., p. 135.

The group solidarity that should arise from the realization that slavery is supported by racist attitudes is not actualized to the extent that Nat anticipated. He is troubled by the fact that against his expectations many blacks not only failed to join him but even fought against him, doing so with no feeling of reluctance. Despite his attempts to create black solidarity, most notably in his first sermon, Nat cannot counteract the accumulated effect of racist doctrine. For it is not only the social position of slavery which he must fight with a sense of personal pride; it is also the understanding of the supposed limitations of black people which he must resist with racial pride. As he says in his sermon:

> "Black folk ain't never goin' to be no great nation until they studies to love they own black skin an' the beauty of that skin an' the beauty of them black hands that toils so hard and black feet that trods so weary on God's earth."[8]

It is a mark of the treachery of the dual injustice, the social institution of slavery and its ideological justification in racist doctrine, that so few of the black people in the area, according to Styron, join in the revolution.

The second source for the revolution is a reservoir of energy upon which Nat draws. This reservoir is suggested in many ways, and it is constituted by whatever in Nat's life lies outside of the immediate conditions of his slave position. He makes contact with it by withdrawing, withdrawing into the woods, into his dreams, into prayer, into fantasies, and into the graveyard. It is not surprising, given the intolerable social position he holds, that Nat should locate the center of his life, the source of its meaning, in areas that white people or the social situation cannot touch. As a young lad standing ready to wait on the table of his master, his attention rests on the spring landscape outside. His sensitivity and love for the woods, for water, and for his morning walks on the trap line suggest that he is oriented to resources which lie outside of the boundaries of the social order. He says at one point, for example:

> But there is a leftover savage part of me that feels very close to my grandmother, and for a couple of years I am drawn irresistibly back

8. Ibid., p. 311.

to the graveyard, and often I steal away from the big house during the hot break after midday dinner, as if seeking among all those toppled and crumbling wood markers . . . some early lesson in mortality.[9]

Nat develops an increasing attachment to natural resources, water, the woods, and death, in order to derive energy for his attack on the social structures, the masters, and ideology which oppress him and his people.

The final component of Nat's fund of resources is a transcendent approbation, the command and the approval of God. The act of revolution is made possible when his energy and sense of moral justification join. Deriving most of his theological insights from the prophets and biblical apocalyptic passages, Nat squeezes the existing social order between neglected or feared energies which lie beyond its boundaries and moral judgment that stands above it. As a son of the earth and messenger of the sky he gathers into himself a wide range of possibilities for rejecting and attacking the decaying and evil social structure.

The specifically religious matter that constitutes Nat's self-understanding and his revolutionary move is crucial to the book. In addition to specific biblical references and words, especially from the prophets, Nat is a pastor, even though his credentials are, as Richard Whitehead points out, wholly internal. The most overt expression of Nat's sense of Christianity is his first sermon, a sermon which is supported by a theology of revolution. Nat points out the close biblical identifications between political and religious events, salvation and social-political independence being two sides of the same event in the delivery of the Hebrew people from Egypt. In addition, of course, Nat is, without appearing to notice it, just past thirty years of age, a carpenter, and the leader of a group who is brought to suffering and trial in Jerusalem, a passion complete with spittle. The religious material and identifications are all too clear. A number of countering emphases keep this material from being too heavy. One is the confusion of other motives and interests with Christianity. Lust, hate, and his rhetorical needs affect Nat's

9. Ibid., pp. 131–32.

attention to religion. But more important is the fact that Nat has from the beginning of his account until the end a sense of God's departure. The result of this is a lessening of the importance of fatherly approbation, an increased importance in natural energies which are couched in female images, and the final elevation of Margaret to a transcendent status so that her voice is merged with that of the Lord. The effect is that the specifically religious or Christian material becomes a way of expressing the revolutionary stance; it is not an end in itself.

The goals of the revolution are revenge, catharsis, and reconciliation. Despite Mr. Gray's contentions about the failure of the movement, these goals seem to be achieved, if only on a personal level.

In the black-white situation, saying "yes" to black means saying "no" to white. It is a response in kind to the racial antipathy Nat and his fellows have suffered for so long. Especially in Hark, Nat tries to surface the hatred toward whites which is the negative side of love toward the blacks. Nat has told them many times that "*To draw the blood of white men is holy in God's eyes.*"[10] However, Nat finds it difficult to overlook the fact that some whites are more deserving of this hatred than others, and he is sensitive to whites who are also victims of the white society, the pathetic Brantley, for example, and to whites who are sensitive to the evils of this society, Cobb, Turner, and Margaret Whitehead. This complication greatly enriches Nat's vision, lending a human and tragic element to an otherwise ideological or apocalyptic simplicity.

Catharsis is another goal of the revolution. Killing has sexual coloration, as Nat imagines several times spending himself by hurting and stabbing white women. At one point he imagines throwing himself on a white woman he has seen in town, "repaying her pity by crushing my teeth against her mouth until the blood ran in rivulets upon her cheeks. . . ."[11] Rape and blood-lust are epitomized in Will, Nat's opposite, who is all unrestrained fury. However, Nat, who has lived these matters in fantasy and idea, is unable to kill in reality, and it is only Margaret, whom he had desired in a more reciprocal, sexual way, that he can kill; she becomes a sacri-

10. Ibid., p. 410.
11. Ibid., p. 265.

ficial victim of his need to establish himself against Will's threats as the group's rightful leader.

The reconciliation which is desired is the new creation on the other side of the combat, a black nation. Although this goal is the most shadowy, Nat seems to have in mind not only the destruction of the present order but the wedding of the earth and sky in the righteous people. Since this goal is the most remote, it slips easily into a private vision, and it becomes for Nat the reconciliation of himself with the heavens through his joining Margaret, a heavenly figure.

Nat's confession, then, is a working out of all that has happened to clarify for himself the occasion, sources, and goals of his revolution. The occasion is the degeneration and evil of the white, oppressive society. The sources are energies which reside outside of that society, energies expressed predominantly in nature imagery and called forth by a transcendent imperative. The goals are social in intention, but they provoke in actuality internal goals rendered primarily in sexual imagery as tension, spending, and reconciliation.

II

Although in his first novel William Styron seems to be rehearsing themes that are commonly associated with Southern writing, especially the portrayal of a decadent present juxtaposed with a memorable but irretrievable past, it may be possible to see already in this early work an alternative to the static vision. Although Styron's interest in re-creative powers which may overturn the present and bring in a refreshing future are shared to some degree by other Southern writers, by Faulkner's faith in the resource of the earth or of black people or by Flannery O'Connor's spiritually militant Francis Tarwater, the act of overthrowing the present in the name of the future has become an increasingly central moment in his corpus, and his emphasis on revolution distinguishes Styron's writing not only from the main emphasis of other Southerners but from that of the major portion of recent American fiction as well.

As we can see in the fiction of authors brought together for this study, the future or past seem to be abandoned for the sake of the present, and militant or aggressive acts seem to be exchanged for quietism. In Powers's novel, Urban turns from his sparring with his world and embarks on a mystifying retreat. De Vries's characters increasingly retreat from realities beyond, behind, or ahead of them, and they settle for the sure, though limited, ground of their own often battered selves. Updike's characters commonly are preoccupied with the past, but they do not try forcefully to reinstate it; they appropriate it in order to be refreshed to face or accept the present. And Malamud's characters tend to end their grasping for something not yet given in order to actualize potentials that lie at hand. The ending of *The Fixer* represents, perhaps, a startling change, as Yakov is prepared to strike out at the existing order. But this ending seems not to be totally consistent with the body of that novel, and the act is not committed within Bok's real world. Despite this possible exception, the pervasive emphasis in this literature is on, to use John Knowles's title, *A Separate Peace*, a withdrawal from a disappointing world and the actualizing of what yet remains of the private or internal life in the present.

These writers are fairly indicative of the interests of American writers in the fifties and sixties. The characters that people this fiction are deeply disappointed by their worlds, but rather than attack they settle for what little is left, potential that resides in the self or in an intimate relationship with someone similarly situated. The mood of this literature tends to be passive and quietistic, although we may be able to expect, given the tone of present times, that our fiction will turn from the private turmoils and separate peaces of the writers in this study toward attitudes epitomized by the black movement and its literature, social engagement and political revolution.

It may be that William Styron has anticipated in the corpus of his writing a trend that will distinguish the fiction of the seventies from that of the preceding two decades. However typical the shift of his emphasis may be, I think the shift is there, and I would suggest, by placing a consideration of his work at the end of this study, that it is a shift which may have implications ranging beyond his work alone. I would also like to suggest that Styron's increasing emphasis on revolution finds an arresting parallel in contemporary religious debate, for it is true that, regardless of the reason, whether lying in real needs within the actual world or propelled internally by deficiencies or resources within each community, the themes and attitudes of revolution mark recent religious discussions as they are beginning, perhaps, to characterize our literature, and the parallels between Styron's vision and these discussions are worth illuminating. The fact that religion is often an important part of his character's worlds or self-understandings makes this comparison a necessity.

Although *Lie Down in Darkness*[12] (1951), is temporally limited by its focus on the events of one day, the day of Peyton Loftis's funeral, the narrator or implied author moves in the work with great freedom. He shifts the point of view often, from the very rare second person point of view in the opening to the first person narration of almost the whole of the last long chapter. And the material he gives us, noteworthily the bulk of the last chapter, is not always determined by the thoughts or memories of the characters who are involved in the funeral. The effect of this technique is to lift the reader above the action, thought, and characters of the book to view a total picture. This picture, although not entirely in black and white, juxtaposes death and rebirth, sadness and joy, despair and hope.

In the forefront of the picture stands the Loftis family, especially Peyton and her parents, Helen and Milton. The three are locked together in a hate-love relationship which keeps them from having any fruitful relationships with other people. What is arresting is the fact that the three need each other so much. As in *The Ballad of the Sad Cafe* or in *The Violent Bear It Away*, the vortex of this triangular interdependence creates such a centripetal force that each member is both a victim and a perpetrator of violence by which he reduces, and is reduced by, the others. The effect of this relationship is clearly seen in Peyton's inability to live outside of her family in New York City. But before the ending of the book it is quite apparent that Peyton desires to arouse her father's lust and her

12. William Styron, *Lie Down in Darkness* (Indianapolis: Bobbs-Merrill Co., Inc., 1951).

mother's anger, that Helen needs Peyton as a hate-object and Milton as an occasion for female suffering, and that Milton wants to feel castrated by Helen, as the pastor's wife observes, and to possess Peyton. The fact that all three overestimate the importance of each other does not alleviate the tension, since they cling to each other not because each deserves the hate or the love he receives but because all three are, as Peyton so desperately feels it, drowning.

The three are drowning, however, not as isolated victims. The world around them is a deeply troubled one; the society offers no meaningful goals or offices; people are terribly weakened by influences beyond their control, especially influences from their pasts; there is no spiritual resource to which people can at moments of distress turn; and there is beyond or behind their worlds no supportive meaning or ameliorating will. The surrounding context of this family's life, then, is no less violent and tortured than they: the bland, silly, or distorted people presented at several parties, parties at the club, at the Cavalier homecoming, at Peyton's wedding, and at the intellectual soirees in New York City; the land disfigured by gas tanks, buildings in disrepair, and refuse; and the global situation epitomized by the bomb dropped on Japan on the day of Peyton's suicide. The surrounding society and world seem to be drowning no less than the Loftis family.

Much as in *The Sound and the Fury*, on the fringes of these foreground figures stand the black people of the Loftis household and the town. They are helpful, as is the young black man who picks Milton up after he has fallen in Charlottesville, sympathetic, as is Ella who genuinely mourns Peyton's death, not because it constitutes the loss of some object she needs, as the death signifies a loss to Helen and Milton, but because of the suffering of the child herself, and they are joyful, since the day of Peyton's funeral is the advent of Daddy Faith.

The advent and message of Daddy Faith are important because they confirm what is suggested throughout the book; he tells his people that the society which has oppressed them and caused them suffering, an oppression and suffering which links his people to the slaves in Egypt, is under judgment and is in the process of destruction. Black people are those who will remain and who can be comforted in this time, since they are not the perpetrators of violence, the results of which are now being visited upon the age.

This picture, juxtaposing sadness and joy, death and rebirth, is, as I have said, not done only in black and white. There is some overlapping, and this lends subtlety to the contrast. For one thing, Daddy Faith is from the North, and the North suggests in this work a place of death. In addition, the North, while being an enervating spiritual wilderness, is the home of Peyton's Jewish husband, Harry, who, not without faults and disturbing needs of his own, seems to marry Peyton for more than her body and to love her despite her distressing acts. Finally, an overlapping is accomplished in the figure of the Reverend Carey Carr.

It is somewhat surprising to find in the Styron corpus a pastor with as much integrity as Carr. Although he is a bit delicate, effeminate, overweight, and uncertain in his vocation, he is a long way from the clergy in *The Confessions of Nat Turner* and from the cruel caricature of the Reverend Norman Vincent Peale in *Set This House on Fire*. Carr seems to have a fairly good relationship with his wife, who is one of the strongest of the white characters in the book; he is not uncritical toward Helen; and he avoids the mistake of becoming a social busybody rather than a pastor or of becoming an uplifted or disdainful spiritual judge. Of course, he is finally ineffective, but in a day when the clergy of fiction tend to distort the spiritual values which they ought to clarify, Carey Carr looks rather good. The effect of this important minor character is to keep the juxtaposition from being too simplistic. Beyond this literary effect, it suggests that in the world of the Peytons there are real spiritual resources which those in distress are not able to receive.

There is little that is revolutionary in the attitudes or acts of characters in this early novel, but the conditions are quite clearly laid down. Of central importance is the feeling that the present situation is an impossible one. It is a dead and stifling burden, as Helen and Milton are, who deny Peyton any freedom to have her own life. As Peyton puts it several times, it is not that these people constitute a lost generation but that they are losing or killing their children. This feeling is not simply a problem of communication between generations, but it indicates, rather, Styron's sensitivity for potential that is being oppressed, for a present that threatens to kill the future. On the fringes stand the joys and genuine sufferings of the blacks. By locating a potential which the present situation threatens to destroy, Styron sets up the possibility of characters turning against or overthrowing the present, the oppressors, in the name of the young, the joyful, and the oppressed.

Quite clearly oppression and rebellion are central experiences for the principal characters of *The Long March*[13] (1952). And as in *Lie Down in Darkness* a potential is recognized in Jews and blacks that others lack. Primarily this potential lies in a sensitivity to oppression and in an ability to identify with people who suffer.

Although it is not told in the first person, Culver is closer to the narrator than Mannix. The result of this proximity is that Culver is presented as a character objectively contrasted with Mannix, but the proximity of the narrator to him allows us to participate in Culver's attitudes towards Mannix, his admiration, envy, and anger toward him.

The problem suggested by the experience of these two men is the elusiveness of the enemy. They and the other Marines feel they are unjustly treated, but, just as the soldiers are fighting an "Aggressor Enemy" who is an illusion, who is never seen, these Marines are put upon by a hostile force they cannot locate. In this situation Culver tends to tolerate what is hostile or to flee from it into the detached beauty of his dreams and memories. However, this tolerance and flight become increasingly difficult in the course of the work, especially in his experience of the terrible accident at the beginning and the suffering of the cruelly senseless march in the middle of the work. Still, Culver is too conditioned by his successful, middle-class life as a budding lawyer in New York to take the accident seriously, although at first it makes him sick, and to support Mannix's resistance toward the perpetrator of the march, Colonel Templeton. Mannix, however, responds to all of this with rage. Because of his many scars, his close call with death in San

13. William Styron, *The Long March* (New York: Random House, 1952).

Francisco, and his identity as a thirty-year-old Jew, he fights the system at every turn and succeeds, at least to his own satisfaction, in identifying the enemy in the person of the Colonel.

The attitude of Culver is as important for the work as are the stance and actions of Mannix, although the rich imagery associated with Mannix, especially his explicit Christ-likeness and his implicit Promethean defiance, make him as central for the book as he is for Culver's life. Although Culver is more similar to Mannix than to those supporters of the situation who flatter their officers or naturally take on the language and habits of the military, Culver's position is held in question by its juxtaposition with that of the rebellious Jew. When Culver observes Mannix talking with the black maid at the end, he stands apart from the circle of oppressed, suffering, and potentially revolutionary people. He has benefited too much from the way things are to turn against the situation even when he sees its evil. Culver is the sensitive observer who can see the great integrity and strength in Mannix's rebellious stand, but he is tied to memories and dreams which he thinks the system can allow him to actualize despite the injustice, oppression, and horror that he sees around him.

Mannix is, again in Camus's terms, more of a rebel than a revolutionary. His act is more a saying "no" to the present than a saying "yes" to some alternative to the present that lies in the future. But his act of rebellion does have aspects which mark the revolutionary stance, primarily his fixing on enemies which can be attacked and his evaluation, suggested by his compassion for the soldiers and his conversation with the maid at the end, of goods for the sake of which this enemy must be overturned.

The three principal characters of *The Long March*, the observer, the oppressor, and the rebel, find their counterparts in *Set This House on Fire*.[14] The primacy of any one of the three for the work could be argued. Cass is the most dynamic and fascinating character, but it is a mistake to focus attention exclusively on him. Peter Leverett, whose presence begins and ends the book, is more than a narrator; he is a major character and perhaps the principal one. Finally, it could be argued that the most important character is

14. William Styron, *Set This House on Fire* (New York: Random House, 1960).

Mason; without him and his death there would be no story to tell, and Peter and Cass would have little in common; it is Mason, his influence on them, and his violent death that they share, and it could be argued that Peter's narrative is primarily concerned with rendering Mason's character and the fall of his house. But rather than one dominating character, we have three who stand together, oppressor, rebel, and observer, and the effect of their confrontations is to clarify the occasion and goal of revolution.

As observer, Peter seems primarily interested in distinguishing evil from good, but he encounters the two together, painfully mixed. So, Peter sees great good and great evil mixed in America. On the one hand, America is victimized by a sordidness which is, although not always perpetrated consciously, a great evil. In addition, Peter sees in America an attack on natural beauty, the rape of the land, the deflowering of America's innocence, a situation that seems to find its parallel in Mason's treatment of Francesca. Peter is aware of these great evils, and Cass shares that awareness. But these men also know the great beauty of America, and Cass can be almost overcome by a thought of the land's great resources. This contrast Peter and Cass also see in Italy. There are places of beauty and innocence, especially Sambuco, a town unsullied by war and, as we are so often told, close to the sea. But with these good things are great evils, the presence of the American movie company, "The Palacial Villa of Emilio Narduzzo of West Englewood, N.J., U.S.A.," the shocking existence of the impoverished peasants whom even the Italians treat with little more than disdain, and, especially, Mason.

Peter and Cass seem to see evil as an imposition on the good, lower reality being good and upper being evil. This pattern is suggested by other facts such as the preference of Southern to Northern locations, of Sambuco to Paris or of South Carolina and Virginia to New York City and Poughkeepsie, and the position of Cass's basement apartment relative to Mason's quarters above. Similarly, Peter has the experience of realizing that the ground on which he stands at one point during his Aeneas-like trip to his father is fill-dirt that now supports commercial, trivial America and covers over a place where as a boy he had reached wisdom.

This broader interest in good and evil and the picture of evil covering good allow us to see the significance of Cass's change in the plot. First we ought to note that there is great good in Cass, despite his weaknesses and failures. He is the first person Peter meets in Italy who sympathizes with Peter's agony over his accident; he is capable of experiences of great beauty, such as the ecstatic moment in Paris; Poppy, a good woman if there ever was one, loves him; he establishes an unusually beautiful relationship with Francesca; and he shows great compassion toward Michele. But Cass, like America, has had this goodness in him assaulted by events, other people, and himself. He has been an orphan, a tool for terribly vicious white racism, and a mental casualty from fighting in the Pacific. In Sambuco Cass is assaulted and imprisoned by Mason, a situation that is violent to Cass because Mason represents so much that Cass hates, false sophistication, arrogant wealth, and white or American superiority toward dark or non-American people. Mason is very much like the evil crust that seems to cover American life. When Cass can no longer tolerate this assault, having been reduced to the state of Mason's trained seal, he literally casts off this evil crust: he hurls the rapist over the cliff.

In the broader context, Cass's act suggests many things to Peter: the old casting off the new, the South casting off the North, the natural casting off the artificial, the poor casting off the rich, the blacks casting off the whites, the people of other countries casting off American domination. It suggests youth, the feminine, the South, the black, the poor, and the past overthrowing the decayed, the desperately oppressive male, the North, the coercive, the rich, and the present.

Cass and Peter need only recognize, apparently, that this action is a good rather than an evil. Despite the great evils they have experienced, the victims of oppression will arise, as does the victim of Peter's auto accident, and, perhaps, even prevail. The move of Peter as observer, from detachment to support of this act, suggests a move very close to the narrative heart of Styron's fiction, for it represents a shift in orientation from Culver's position in *The Long March*. From a position sympathetic with but unsupportive of rebellion, the narrator moves to complicity in revolution.

Perhaps a reader acquainted with Styron's other work could

THE DYNAMIC OF REVOLUTION

expect, on picking up *The Confessions of Nat Turner*, an enthusias-
tic celebration of a social revolutionary. If that which I have said
so far is true, Styron's narrators seem increasingly fascinated by the
need for revolution, the throwing off of oppression. But it turns out
that this novel, which would potentially be the most affirmative
toward revolutionary acts, casts the social significance of the historical event in an internal and psychological mold. To the degree
that Nat is more concerned with the private reasons for his actions
and with his doubts and frustrations arising from them than in the
basis for the act in the situation within which he and other blacks
live, the work withdraws from the affirmative attitude toward
revolution which Styron's narrators seem increasingly to have expressed.

Black critics of the work[15] have been quick to point out that
Styron's version of Nat Turner's rebellion entirely destroys the
real, revolutionary character of his act. Of course, it is important
for these black critics to maintain that the occasion for the revolution lay in the situation itself, a situation greatly but not entirely
altered in the present, and that Nat was not singular in his antipathy
for whites. Styron, with his internal focus, seems to put the cause
of the revolution within Nat and to see his attitudes as exceptional.
There are other matters in the work which Styron's black critics do
not like: that Nat, apparently a married man, is presented as given
to a sex life of masturbation, homosexuality, and dreams of white
girls; that Nat seems to despise blacks less gifted than himself and
tends to use them in the revolution for his own purposes; and that
Styron locates the evils of slavery in poor, uneducated slave-owners,
suggesting that there were "good" masters. They feel that Styron
has taken a strong, courageous, and morally or religiously motivated man, a man who brought to the surface what was universally
felt by slaves, and has turned him into an intellectual or neurotic
snob.

Given the development in his corpus and given the nature of his
material, it is surprising, perhaps, that Styron has transmuted social,
revolutionary events into individual and psychological experiences.

15. Cf. John Henrik Clark, ed., *William Styron's Nat Turner: Ten Black
Writers Respond* (Boston: Beacon Press, 1968).

133

Given, too, the interest in social revolution characteristic of our times and the sensitive question of group self-identity among blacks, it may be unfortunate that he treated in this manner a moment of black revolution. Although his black critics tend to neglect those elements in Styron's Nat Turner which speak of a more general need and potential for revolution, their offense at his treatment is understandable.

Rather than impute his retelling to racism or ignorance of slave conditions, as his black critics tend to do, I would suggest that Styron is moving, with this work, toward a more mythic vision of revolution. What is noteworthy is not the interest in the psychological aspect but in the rather stylized juxtaposition of mythic elements: male and female, sky and earth, land and water. The psychological and the sociological aspects of revolution are directed toward this mythlike rendering of forces by which individuals and groups are determined. Although it is found in his other works, Styron's growing interest in myth appears here to be especially strong. In fact, I would suggest that by moving from the historical and sociological significance of Nat Turner to a more psychologically preoccupied confessional fiction, Styron is less interested in revolution for one person or one group or one time than in a revolutionary dynamic that governs persons and groups, societies and history.

III

The effects of the present revolutionary climate can be detected in current religious debate quite readily. Fortified by a theology of hope articulated especially by Wolfhart Pannenberg and Jürgen Moltmann, a theology stimulated by the work of Marxist Ernst Bloch, *Das Prinzip Hoffnung*, reflection on social, economic, and political revolution marked the religious scene during the second half of the sixties as the "death of God" debate marked the first half of the decade.[16]

16. Cf. Jürgen Moltmann, *Religion, Revolution, and the Future*, trans. M. Douglas Meeks (New York: Charles Scribner's Sons, 1969), Ernst Feil and Rudolf Weth, eds., *Diskussion zur Theologie der Revolution* (Mains: Chr. Kaiser Verlag, 1969), Jacques Ellul, *Violence: Reflections from a Christian Perspective* (New York: Seabury Press, 1969), James H. Cone,

Religious interest in revolution arises from several considerations, some of which we already have discussed. The most obvious is the loss of sacramental potential in the present situation. Because vocation has increasingly become a problem and because the meaninglessness or inappropriateness of the word "God" has been experienced in so many moments of collective and personal life, the present is viewed as a spiritual wasteland. As the present was felt by some "death of God" theologians to be a point of transition to a badly needed new form of religiousness (Altizer and Rubenstein, especially), so the debate on revolution appears stimulated by a sense of extremity reached by the present economic-social-political structure which has debased life, jeopardized, if not destroyed, freedom, and oppressed minorities in the industrialized hemisphere and majorities in the nations of the third world. The "death of God" debate and the current discussion of revolution have at least this in common: a sense that the present constitutes a crisis or a transition period and the sense that the present is devoid of sacramental potential.

A second consideration central to the current revolutionary interest is the high evaluation of a disregarded or dishonored good. With the increased sensitivity to evils within the present situation there has developed an increased sensitivity to a good which this evil dominates. Primarily referred to as the "poor," the oppressed or suffering good is often extended to include minority groups, personal freedom, emotional or sexual spontaneity, women, and the earth. An economic-social-political structure which is believed to have become increasingly self-perpetuating and profane is seen to dominate, repress, and exploit a good or a set of goods which needs to be vindicated.

These two interrelated considerations, an evil structure and an oppressed good, are fortified by two considerations which are more theological or mythic in character. The first of these is expressed in the theology of hope and the second in the mythic conflicts characteristic of biblical moments of creation and re-creation.

Black Theology and Black Power (New York: Seabury Press, 1969), and M. Richard Shaull, *Encounter with Revolution* (New York: Association Press, 1955).

The theology of hope is, like Marxism, oriented to the future. Albert Camus noted that the revolutionary, unlike the rebel, is willing to injure the present in eager anticipation of a better future. In Matthew Arnold's terms, Camus's rebel is Hellenic in nature while the Christian and the Marxist are Hebraic. The theology of hope fortifies dissatisfaction with the present by emphasizing the religious man's knowledge of and occasional participation in the end, in a time when things will be other than they now are. This knowledge and participation always loosen him from the present and stimulate him to alter those aspects of the present which defy the future and to actualize that potential in the present which speaks of the future. Becoming now what one day we shall be, a process known on the personal level as sanctification, is seen to have implications for one's relation to collective life and is even seen as a necessary ingredient within that life. The future so understood religiously is qualitatively and not quantitatively different from the present. It is not that the future is merely an extension of the present: it is something new; it is related to God's kingdom, and thus stands in judgment on the present.

The second mythic or theological consideration is the recollection or rehearsal of conflicts in the past. The Bible includes several: the conflicts associated with the delivery of the oppressed Hebrews from Egypt; the conflict of Joshua, the delivery of the promised land from the hands of unholy men; the conflicts of the judges with those evil forces which had been allowed to overrun the holy land and dominate the valued people; the conflicts of the prophets with an increasingly profane and exploitive social-political situation; the conflict of Jesus, especially in the Gospel of Mark, with demonic powers which have taken over the world and the present age; and the picture of the power of God in Revelation as the terrible Rider on the White Horse (Rev. 19:11 ff.). These examples indicate that religious thought that is shaped by reflection on the Bible can easily regard the religious man's relation to an evil situation as a militant one.

One central question in all of this is similar to the question which has arisen throughout this study, the question of the relation of religious matters to matters which lie outside its domain. What relations do the conflicts in the Bible and conflicts implied by the theology of hope have to secular revolutionary thought and movements in our day?

It should be quite clear that the material relating the conflicts of the Exodus and the conflicts connected with the promised land is a material presenting a set of events and actions which are qualitatively different from those which normally occur. This could also be said of the set of events and actions described in association with the life, death, and resurrection of Jesus. Most obviously, things of a highly unusual nature occurred or were accomplished. More subtly, the sets of events or actions celebrated in such material are unlike usual actions and occurrences because they are not imprisoned in time. A Jewish family celebrating Passover is as much in the presence of these realities as were those who came out of Egypt; a Christian who participates in the Eucharist is, in traditional understanding, in the presence of the real Christ. The Exodus is not locked to a historical time; the presence of Christ is not confined to a period of history at the opening of the Christian era. The relation of the Gospels' accounts of the person and work of Jesus, or of the careers of the judges as they are interpreted by the Deuteronomic theologian-historian, or of Joshua or of Moses and the Exodus to actual occurrences, the actual life of Jesus or the origins of Israel as a unified people, are highly problematic. Just as problematic, therefore, is the relation of these materials to present history. In a word, if the question of the relation of the Jesus of the Gospels to the historical Jesus is a difficult one, the relation of the Jesus of the Gospels to present history is *a fortiori* not immediately apparent or direct. The question of myth's relation to history is a crucial one in current debate concerning a Christian's response to social, political, or economic revolution.

The second major problem derives from the use of the prophets as paradigmatic for a religiously motivated participation in revolutionary activity. The importance of Jesus is also to be mentioned, since he can be taken as, among other things, standing in the tradition of the prophets speaking against the structures of his world in the name of the past, the wilderness to which he retreats, and the future, the kingdom which he introduces. The importance of the prophets for this debate is extended by the fact that they were quite central to that attempt to relate Christian theology to social problems at the end of the last and the beginning of the present century, an attempt associated with names like Walter Rauschenbusch and Shailer Mathews and called the "social gospel" movement. The problem here is that the prophets are primarily identified with the word, and whatever actions they initiated came more from their interest in illustrating or making vivid that word than in participating in political or social revolution. A recent attempt has been made to see the historical Jesus as a revolutionary whom the Gospel writers reshaped as a pacifist in order to make him more acceptable to the Roman world.[17] But this attempt, while pointing to a number of problematic items in the Gospels, is vulnerable to all the questions connected with establishing a clear picture of the historical Jesus. But more importantly, the sword of Jesus and of the prophets before him was the sword of the word.

The matter of speaking against social and political evils rather than acting as a revolutionary against them has aroused a good bit of debate, and the two positions can be seen in Richard Shaull's attitudes as contrasted with those of Jacques Ellul. The disagreement is a rather urgent one because the alternative answers are unattractive. On the one hand, participation in social revolution propels one to acts of violence which have a momentum built into them, a momentum which draws the participant along, threatening his freedom.[18] For a Christian theologian this loss of freedom or loss of responsibility is an unattractive consequence. No more attractive is the prospect of a religious life expressed in inflammatory words but not in violent deeds, an apparently disincarnate religiousness. The problem is an old one, how to be in the world without being a part of it and how yet to be in the world and not apart from it.

The religious debate concerning revolution, then, is marked by a sensitivity to evils within existing structures, a desire to redeem or liberate oppressed or violated goods, an awareness of the rela-

17. S. G. F. Brandon, *Jesus and the Zealots* (Manchester: Manchester University Press, 1967).
18. Cf. Ellul, *Violence,* especially pp. 96–97.

tion of the Christian to a future which illuminates the evils of the present, and a rehearsing of biblical moments of violent liberation of people, land, or religious objects which had been victimized by the power of evil. Embedded in the debate is a set of problems arising from what we have seen as a recurring theme in the fiction and the religious thought we have considered, the tension between religious and nonreligious matters. Here the tension arises from the relation of myth to history and the relation of religious word to public action.

The current religious debate concerning revolution makes clear an attempt to keep religion from a preoccupation with that in its life which removes it from historical realities. As the "social gospel" was a call away from otherworldly interests to the actual problems in the present, the debate over revolution is calculated to correct the tendency of churches toward detachment from and irrelevancy to what is happening in the economic, political, and social world. This tendency is as much a mark of recent fiction as it is of religion in our time.

A "separate peace" apart from the conflicts that mark a society is more characteristic of the stance of characters or narrators in recent fiction than is engagement in such conflicts. And patterns of escape, as in the fiction of Kerouac, Kesey, Percy, Coover, Barth, Vonnegut, and Brautigan, are more recurring than the patterns of involvement and conflict. "Lighting out for the territory" or "a separate peace" are themes which mark our fiction as much as, or perhaps even more than, current theology. But it is significant that the tendency toward separation is endemic to both. When nothing of separation exists one no longer seems to have fiction or religion.

In this context the fiction of William Styron stands out as revealing oppressed goods which must be redeemed from existing evil structures and as including, especially in *The Confessions of Nat Turner,* preoccupation with the myths of conflict which relate both to the beginning and the end. I feel that Styron's corpus suggests a move from preoccupation with the rebel to celebration of the revolutionary. This move may indicate something about the future of the form. As we have moved through this fiction from Powers to Styron we have seen an increasing restlessness, rebellion, and finally

revolution in the face of increasingly difficult and intractable problems. I believe that the present revolutionary interests in our society
may easily encourage our fiction to leave the precious, separate
peace, to end the quiet, waiting endurance of evil, and even to go
beyond the resistance of the rebel to the violent acts and attitudes
of the revolutionary.

Conclusion:

Abraham's Third Sons

At the close of the Introduction, I promised to return in the Conclusion to the problem which underlies the question at issue in each of the five works of fiction, an underlying problem which causes or aggravates the several particular ones. That underlying difficulty is the separation of religious acts, feelings, and ideas from nonreligious ones and the division between the private and public domains. The worlds of Urban, Wanderhope, Peter Caldwell, Bok, and Nat Turner are taxing because they are divided. Urban is awakened to the rift between the Church and the non-Church; Don Wanderhope tries but fails to come to some understanding of the relation of God's power or will to other causes; Peter Caldwell cannot resolve, as George appears to, the conflict between the spiritual world and the world of human weakness, suffering, and death; Yakov Bok cannot reconcile the history of Jewish suffering to the traditional affirmation that God acts in history; and Nat Turner is distressed over the uncertain connection between God's wrath and the violence of revolutionary acts.

The problem in each case is solved in a personal way. The problem becomes an occasion for Father Urban's spiritual retreat, for Wanderhope's celebration of immediate, human joys, for Peter's reaffirmation of his father's wisdom, for Bok's clarification of his Jewish identity through resistance, and for Nat Turner's sense of fulfillment in and through the presence of the ascended girl. The problem is not explicitly solved. Rather, the problem produces a pain, a pain constituting the discipline the narrator or character undergoes on the way to gaining a new understanding of the word

CONCLUSION

"I." If the problem is solved at all it is so by the works themselves, establishing as they do a middle ground between the separated components, the private-religious and the public-nonreligious domains.

Theologians tend to aggravate this separation either by rejecting it or by taking a stand on one of the two sides and interpreting the other side in its terms. They reject the problem because it smacks of dualism, of Manichaeism, of a resulting irrelevancy and preciousness for religious life and thought, and of an implied rejection or disdain for the temporal, the physical, or the secular. Consequently, they tend to take up a position on one side or on the other, insisting that all of life can be understood in terms derived from the religious domain or by insisting that anything of value in Jewish or Christian religion can be fully expressed, without significant remainder, in statements which can be understood and accepted by any person sufficiently sensitive to logical or empirical verifications.

Theologians who use religious categories to embrace the nonreligious domain see the decision of God or the universal implications of the church to be so undeniable in implication that all people, regardless of their attitude toward religious matters, are spoken of in religious terms. If people do not speak of themselves in ways similar to those by which these theologians refer to them, it is said that these are people who are without their knowledge partakers in the effect of God's decisions or are potentially or anonymously members of Christ's church. Karl Barth wrote, for example:

> . . . we cannot at all reckon in a serious way with *real* "outsiders," with a "world come of age," but only with a world which *regards* itself as of age (and proves daily that it is precisely not that). Thus the so-called "outsiders" are really only "insiders" who have not yet understood and apprehended themselves as such.[1]

Under the decision of God to be with man, all men, regardless of their relation to religious matters and institutions, are to be understood as "insiders" and "outsiders" at the same time, to the degree that they are or are not related to the sources and consequences of

1. Karl Barth, *The Humanity of God*, trans. John Newton Thomas (Richmond: John Knox Press, 1960), pp. 58–59.

that decision. Similarly, a Roman Catholic theologian with great obligation to the specific Christian structure says:

> Christianity encounters the man of the extra-Christian religion not merely as a non-Christian pure and simple, but as one who, in one respect or another, can and must be considered already as an anonymous Christian. It would be false to consider the pagan a man untouched by God's grace and truth.[2]

Presumably, Karl Rahner would include under the category of "pagan" those members of American society who stand in no observable or conscious relation to the church. For theologians of this sort, all men are to be seen in terms of categories derived from a religious context. What appear as two worlds are really united by the power of divine decision-making or by the real authority of the church.

Working from the other side, theologians have at times attempted to exhaust the meaning of the language of religion by translating it into parallel philosophical terms. One example is provided by those who, influenced by Charles Hartshorne, use modes of process philosophy as a way of talking about God's relation to the world so that the relationship is free from the arbitrariness and authority suggested by a church theology or a theology of grace. Hartshorne considers it possible to speak freely about God's relation to the world within the limits of nonreligious language, and within those limits he makes his case for a God who is both immanent and transcendent, who transcends himself, and who is passive to and enlarged by the world with which he is continuous.[3] This way of speaking was amplified by one of Hartshorne's students, Bernard Loomer, who, insisting that the Christian faith can be expressed without significant remainder in the categories of process metaphysics, concluded that "God is material being, a process with an enduring structure. . . ."[4] In such a framework as this, the forgive-

2. Karl Rahner, "Christianity and Non-Christian Religions" in *The Church: Readings in Theology*, ed. Albert La Pierre, Bernard Verkamp et al. (New York: P. J. Kenedy and Sons, 1963), p. 131.
3. Cf. Charles Hartshorne, *Reality as Social Process* (Boston: Beacon Press and Glencoe, Ill.: Free Press, 1953), especially p. 130.
4. Bernard Loomer, "Neo-Naturalism and Neo-Orthodoxy," *The Journal of Religion* 28, no. 2 (April 1948):82.

CONCLUSION

ness of sins is not a gratuitous act but "is necessary for God's own self-fulfillment";[5] revelation and incarnation are natural facts, since "the world always embodied this divine ordering and this creative process."[6] Similarly, attempts have been made to give complete expression to the meaning of Christian belief in existentialist categories. Shubert Ogden, for example, asserted that "Christian faith is to be interpreted exhaustively and without remainder as man's original possibility of authentic existence as this is clarified and conceptualized by an appropriate philosophical analysis."[7] In this instance, reflection on human existence can provide one with adequate categories to exhaust the meaning of the language of Christianity.

The flaw in both attempts is that they resolve the tension by destroying one side, and they increase the tension within theological communities between orthodox and modern or conservative and liberal without solving the problem. For one, the nonreligious is not taken seriously; it is either an unfortunate degeneration from former belief or an impermanent or incomplete position prior to belief. The nonreligious is always seen in relation to the religious. For the other the religious is not taken seriously; it is at best a resource, as Hartshorne puts it, for "hypotheses."[8] At its worst it constitutes an obscure or outmoded form of human expression.

Nor can the problem be solved by positing some unifying reality behind the two separated components, a reality suggested by the organic, interdependent relations the two parts would be thought of as having with one another. Metaphors are used to describe the organic relationship, the nonreligious and the religious having been seen by Paul Tillich,[9] of course, as being interrelated as question and answer, and theologians influenced by Marx tend to relate the two using the metaphor of soul and body, so that a religious man not involved in social and political realities is religiously disincar-

5. Bernard Loomer, "Christian Faith and Process Philosophy," *The Journal of Religion* 29, no. 3 (July 1949):195.
6. Ibid., p. 198.
7. Shubert Ogden, *Christ Without Myth* (New York: Harper and Brothers, 1961), p. 146.
8. Hartshorne, *Reality as Social Process*, p. 130.
9. Cf. Paul Tillich, *Systematic Theology*, Vol. 1 (Chicago: University of Chicago Press, 1951), especially p. 62.

144

nate. Salt of the earth or leaven of the lump or soul of the body are biblical and theological metaphors by which the present situation of separation between the religious and the nonreligious may be seen as united by the metaphor's missing middle factor, the unifying being or power expressing itself through interdependent poles.

Attempts to denounce the problem as Manichaen, to resolve it by devouring one side with the mouth of the other, or to suggest that the two sides are held in tension by an underlying, unifying being or power fail, I think, to face the situation to which the fiction we have studied bears witness. What we have is a torn world in which two goods are separated from one another, in which two self-enclosed worlds are unrelated.

It may be possible to describe this situation by recalling the tension that existed between the two homes of Abraham's sons, Isaac and Ishmael. Isaac has his home because of the gratuitous and authoritative promise and command of God by which Ishmael was displaced from his privileged seat as Abraham's first son by Isaac, the second born. Not only that, because Sarah felt the deep conflict between the two, she acted to have Ishmael removed from Abraham's tent entirely. Out in the wilderness Ishmael developed his own place, a place not made for him by God's gratuitous election but made by him through his own courage and resourcefulness; he makes the wilderness his home, marries a woman from Egypt, and becomes an expert with the bow.

The two sons of Abraham suggest two arenas, one characterized by the word of God and the other by human creativity. Perhaps these two arenas are still present today: those oriented to Jewish or Christian communities and authorities, those for whom the language of grace is primary, and those who live apart from such communities and authorities and, as did Ishmael, make the best of what lies at hand.

Between these two camps has arisen a sizable number of people who live totally in neither and try to live at times in each. These are third sons of Abraham, refusing to reject the forms of grace and also refusing to violate the integrity of secular enterprise. These people feel in themselves and their worlds components and forces which resist each other and will not be confused. At times such people may try to unite the two sides, but when they do they offend their friends in both camps and they probably fail fully to satisfy themselves, too.

It is predictable and desirable that attempts be made to unify this broken world from either the side of confession or the side of scientific or philosophical creativity. It is predictable that this should go on because people cannot live content before fragments and because they are threatened by a torn world. The attempts are desirable because they reveal at times how much of the two realms overlap. At times, too, they allow us for a moment to live in a sense of wholeness, an experience which satisfies our longing for peace.

While the fiction we have studied witnesses to this problem, it also resolves it. Works of recent fiction can bring subjectivity, including religious elements, into the public, secular domain. And they can point to moments of finality and transcendence in non-religious experience, especially violence, death, human intimacy, and self-identity. But I believe the works of fiction we have studied are most impressive in their exposure of the problem, the rift between religion and nonreligious understandings and expections. The solution to the problem lies in a newly acceptable, realized "I," personal peace and significance.

These works of fiction, then, are third sons of Abraham. They testify to a divided world, and rather than heal this division or rather than reject one side for the sake of the other, their narrators and characters face the problem, take something into themselves from both sides, and achieve new meaning in the word "I" despite or because of the problem's force. The direction in which they are taken for achieving this new sense of "I" is toward retreat and silence.

As Ihab Hassan has pointed out, a work of literature may be oriented toward one of two kinds of silence.[10] Perhaps these kinds can be clarified by a reaction to Frank Kermode's *The Sense of an Ending.*[11] Kermode's thesis is that the fiction-maker finds himself

10. Ihab Hassan, *The Literature of Silence: Henry Miller and Samuel Beckett* (New York: Alfred A. Knopf, 1967).
11. Frank Kermode, *The Sense of an Ending: Studies in the Theory of Fiction* (New York: Oxford University Press, 1967).

in the midst of events and structures that are discrete, ununified. In this position in the middle of things he begins to give order to confusion by his fictive powers, giving relationships to objects and events, relating them to one another, to a beginning, and more importantly, to an end. Fictions, then, provide the artist and the reader with concords, and without such imaginative concords man lives as a victim of chaos.

Kermode describes the interactions between the imagination and undifferentiated times or unconnected objects and events, between the fiction-maker and the confusion around him, as an essentially sexual one. He says, speaking of Sartre's *La Nausée*:

> Contingency is nauseous and viscous; it has been suggested that the figure is ultimately sexual. This is unformed matter, *materia, matrix*; Roquentin's is ultimately the form-giving male role.[12]

This sexual metaphor should not be surprising. Kermode has behind him an unrecognized plethora of myths.

The problem with Kermode's study is not this mythlike understanding of the relation of the creative artist to the undifferentiated or unrealized potential of his internal or external experience. The problem arises from the incompleteness of Kermode's myth, for the interaction between potential and formative power is more extended than he suggests.

One creative act may be to tear down those forms which have become self-protective or self-sufficient, to reduce everything to the "nauseous and viscous" once again. The religious man is not so afraid of chaos as Kermode seems to be, and he does not always take chaos as the natural situation, as Kermode seems to do. Getting down to potential and undifferentiatedness requires discipline, and the religious man had included for him in his calendar times when such work or discipline had to be taken on. In contrast to religious people, Kermode sees chaos as a given, and he dislikes it, as he also dislikes Alain Robbe-Grillet and William Burroughs. For this reason he is unappreciative of the discipline required for the writing and reading of such authors as these. (Hassan would include the work of Samuel Beckett and Henry Miller.) The disci-

12. Ibid., p. 136.

pline of a fiction may be one which moves the reader to disunity, to the chaos before the word.

But there is another silence suggested by religious life and thought. It is the silence not before but after the word. That silence is thought of generally as feminine, too. Not only is the water or the potential feminine; the feminine enters again, later. In addition to being formless potential, the feminine is also the highest and most perfect form to which the male structures point: wisdom for the Proverbs, Beatrice for Dante, and the silence of the mothers reached by Melville's Ishmael in the midst of the whale herd. Kermode is too preoccupied with the form-giving act to seek out this feminine principle on the other side of fictive forms, the silence of perfect concord.

The silence to which our five, male fiction writers direct us is of both kinds. First we must go through the discipline of confronting the brokenness of what is sometimes taken as a unified world; we move with the characters primarily to a recognition of the distance between religious and nonreligious things. But we also move to the other silence, to the image in which divisions are healed and transcended, the silence of retreat, of childlike candor and grace, of the irretrievable joys of youth, of a unified people, and of transcendent forgiveness. But the silence is not limited to such images. It is also the experience that separated structures in our conscious worlds give testimony to a totally disunified world of the imagination in its sheer potentiality, and it is the experience that beyond our conscious world of structures or events separated or in conflict with each other is the quiet of their imagined reconciliation and unity. Chaos and unity are experiences of the mind and spirit to which the discipline of fiction writing and reading can direct us. Such aesthetic experiences are parallel to moments in religious life. When such moments are included in fiction, as they are in the works we have studied, the two kinds of experiences complicate one another. It has been to clarify the nature of this complicated interpenetration that this study has been carried on.

The role of the imagination in revealing to us the confusion resulting from separated parts and the peace in reaching a personal solution to the problem is of central importance for our society.

That role should be recognized and highly regarded. We need quasi-religious forms. Recent fiction is only one, however significant it may be. We need more, and we need more that are public. We need more and more meaningful quasi-religious celebrations and rituals to complement the literary word. But we must not, with our participation in such forms, forget the integrity, primacy, and probable irreconcilability of those components whose separation grants power and meaning to quasi-religious forms of word and ritual by which, perhaps, our worlds can be at moments seen as one.

Type, 10 on 12 and 9 on 10 Times Roman
Display, Craw and Helvetica